Angelic Visitations
and
Supernatural Encounters

Michael Van Vlymen

Copyright © 2014 Michael Van Vlymen

All rights reserved. This book is protected by the copyright laws of the United States of America. This book may not be reprinted or copied for commercial use or profit. The use of short passages or page copying for personal use or group study is permitted and encouraged.

Angelic Visitations and Supernatural Encounters is available at www.amazon.com and also at bookstores and book distributors worldwide.

ISBN:13 : 978-1495414237
ISBN-10: 149541423x

DEDICATION

This book is dedicated to all those who are hungry for the deep things of God. To all those who desire to live a life less ordinary, I pray this record of events will inspire you. Also, I dedicate this book to my family, whose lives and stories are also reflected in these pages. Thank you for allowing me to share a little bit of your lives. Most importantly this book is dedicated to the Lord Jesus who is the Giver of all good gifts. Thank You..

MICHAEL VAN VLYMEN

INTRODUCTION

This is a great time to be a believer! We are living at a time that is unique in human history. Everyone here has been hand-picked by God Himself for this time, to fulfill their role in the work of the final harvest. Everyone has an important part to play. No one has to be left out of this adventure!

God is doing all the stuff we read about years ago in Sunday School. Only this time the angels aren't flannel graph and the visitations are up close and personal. The really great thing about all this is that this is for everyone! God is using every day, ordinary in the pews people to do the most remarkable supernatural feats. And He is doing it all over the world!

The events recorded in this book are not meant to simply *entertain* anyone. They are meant to serve as a catalyst and inspire you! They are meant to pull you into the deeper things so that you can write your own story of visitations! They are meant to deepen your desire for the Lord and His kingdom.

Are Angelic Visitations and Supernatural Encounters for everyone? Absolutely yes, for everyone!

ANGELIC VISITATIONS AND SUPERNATURAL ENCOUNTERS

CONTENTS

	Acknowledgments	i
Chapter 1	Brace Yourself	3
Chapter 2	Our Supernatural Heritage	9
Chapter 3	The Sounds of Heaven	19
Chapter 4	The Blessings of God	31
Chapter 5	Let There Be Light	45
Chapter 6	Angels Appearing as Men	53
Chapter 7	Angels in the Spirit Realm	61
Chapter 8	Dreams and Visions	87
Chapter 9	Moving in the Spirit Realm	101
Chapter 10	Dark Things	117
Chapter 11	The Strange and Wonderful	131
Chapter 12	Supernatural Resources	147

ACKNOWLEDGMENTS

As these angelic visitations and supernatural encounters began to manifest in my life, my family, and in my home, I gained a lot of understanding from a host of people who have lived this lifestyle of constant communion with God. I would like to say thank you to those who have helped me and have impacted me either directly or indirectly, significantly.

Special thanks to my parents, Marvin and Cathy Van Vlymen and to my in-laws, Lube and Angelina Rusomaroff. Also, thank you to my wife Gordana, without whose love and support this book would not have been possible.

Thank you also to all the people whose names I never knew who have prayed for me at churches and conferences..

1

BRACE YOURSELF

To one who has faith, no explanation is necessary. To one without faith, no explanation is possible.
                    St. Thomas Aquinas

We are in a wondrous time! I know that you can feel it in the air around you. It seems that nearly every prophet of God on the Earth today is saying the same thing, that the veil between the seen and the unseen is thinner than it has ever been. Those who have desire to see past the veil will not be disappointed. Justin Abraham of the Company of Burning Hearts in Wales, says that desire and honor are very important keys to unlock the supernatural things of God in your life.

I want to encourage you to throw everything you have into this quest. Claim your birthright established by the Lord Jesus Christ, and take a sword to all the obstructions that would stand in your way! All of Heaven is cheering you on! As you read through the coming chapters and learn of visions and visitations, Heavenly experiences and Kingdom exploits, please lay hold of the fact that *you can have even greater!*

It is my desire and prayer to the Lord that everyone who desires to walk in these things and use them for the glory of the Lord receive exponentially greater. You can live a life full of adventure and excitement in Christ that is tailor made just for you. As you read, if you find that something stirs you tell the Lord "I want that!", "I'm willing to do that!" Be completely honest with the Lord. He knows your heart and your desires. He gave you this hunger you feel for this intimate relationship you are seeking. It's more than OK that your desires are the things of the Kingdom of Heaven!

Pursue love, and earnestly desire the spiritual gifts, especially that you may prophesy. (1 Corinthians 14:1)

If then you have been raised with Christ, seek the things that are above, where Christ is, seated at the right hand of God. (Colossians 3:1)

To be a habitation of God as your life's goal is a worthy pursuit. Jamie Galloway of East Gate Church in Westchester, PA says that being a habitation is a life of constant visitation. Don't be in fear. Give yourself completely to whatever His will is for you and you will never be sorry.

Bill Johnson of Bethel Church in Redding, CA, says that a testimony carries with it a seed of another similar event or miracle. Any testimony you hear affects you. Every story of angelic visitation or miracle or healing or wonder carries a seed to open that over your life as well.

If you pursue this it will happen. Brace yourself because it's coming. When I began to desire the things of the Kingdom of Heaven, God answered my desire. When I asked Him how to pray, He told me. When I asked Him how to see, He showed me. He withheld nothing from me that I desired in this regard. The reason I'm telling you this is because I want you to know that it's not because I'm "special".

I am not a minister with a ministry. I am not a prophet or an apostle. I am not a pastor or worship leader. I am only a man who is a child of God, a member of His household. I have nothing else that would "qualify" me to receive any special consideration from God. He tells us to pursue spiritual things and then He helps us do as He wills. It's as simple as that. God will do this for you if you desire it.

This book is not just about my story. It's about you. It's about God building faith and causing it to rise up in you, so that you can lay hold of all this and more.

Priming the Pump

In my own life, there were certain things that played an important role in bringing about the manifestation of these encounters with the Kingdom of Heaven. In my book "How to See in the Spirit", I talk about the role the program "It's Supernatural " played in bringing my family into the reality of the supernatural of God. Sid Roth's program shows modern day miracles, signs, wonders, healings, deliverances and more. All these events and stories are researched, documented and recorded to do the exact same thing that I desire to do with this book. To bring about a shift in people's lives is the goal. A shift into a greater reality. My wife Gordana and I, as well as our children, watched practically every episode including the archived shows. You talk about the power of testimony, that will do the job!

We also had fellowship with people who believe in and move in the gifts of the Spirit. We shared testimonies of other people's miracles at the dinner table, over coffee, driving to church, driving home from church. I'm sure you get the idea. We would talk about the power of God at Bible study, we would pray for the manifestation of God's Kingdom to come. (on Earth as it is in Heaven) If you seek a lifestyle of miracles and value the things of God more than anything else, you will be living in that place. What you focus on you connect with. (Be careful little eyes what you see.)

The Resources of Heaven

All of Heaven stands ready to help you. The entire focus of the Lord right now is to bring all to a saving knowledge of Him, to destroy the works of the devil, and to bring us His body into maturity.

The Bible is full of promises that *we are to lay hold of*. The Lord has given us a blood covenant that is irrevocable and completely supernatural in nature. God will bring it to pass if He has spoken it.

God is not a man, that He should lie; neither the son of man, that He should repent; hath He said, and shall He not do it? Or hath He spoken, and shall He not make it good? (Numbers 23:19)

He that spared not His own Son, but delivered Him up for us all, how shall He not with Him also freely give us all things. (Romans 8:32)

For He shall give His angels charge over thee, to keep thee in all thy ways. (Psalms 91:11)

When you encounter angels they won't be disinterested. They are all about doing the will of God. They will help you in any and every way that they can. The Bible also talks about the cloud of witnesses.

Wherefore seeing we are also compassed about with so great a cloud of witnesses, let us lay aside every weight, and the sin which doth so easily beset us, and let us run with patience the race that is set before us. (Hebrews 12:1)

The cloud of witnesses are not bystanders either. All of Heaven plays an important part. Do you think people stop talking to the Lord when they go to Heaven? Of course not.

What is Heaven Doing?

The prophets, the saints, the men in white linen, the living creatures, angels, archangels, the cloud of witnesses all have a part. We all have a mandate to fulfill and the residents of Heaven are a part of the church also. We need to remember that. They do the will of God also and they are very effective allies on our team.

As you experience supernatural things you must obviously have wisdom. You must also be sensitive to the Holy Spirit to lead you and keep you on His path.

Some in the church world think that if you see angels or saints, you are being deceived. Many will mention a verse in the Bible about communication with the dead being forbidden. (Isaiah 8:19) But, what we must consider is the fact that our God is not the God of the dead, but of the living!

He is not the God of the dead, but the God of the living: Ye therefore do greatly err. (Mark 12:27)

If you are seriously pursuing a relationship with God, please take Prophet Bobby Conner's advice. Believe that God has more power to direct you than the devil does to deceive you.

Or what man is there of you, whom if his son ask bread, will he give him a stone? (Matthew 7:9)

Be bold in pursuing the things of God knowing that He Himself is your protector, your strong tower. Be fearless as you go, knowing that you are family. You are members of God's own household. You are seated in Heavenly places in Christ. We really need to remember that death is *not* the door into the Heavenly realms, The Lord Jesus is.

2

OUR SUPERNATURAL HERITAGE

The Wonderful and the Bizarre

Looking at the events of the Old Testament *without* faith, would cause anyone to be challenged to believe. The things that God did with and through His people were *not* things that could be explained by natural means. Constantly God was revealing His power, putting Himself on display so to speak, so that everyone would know beyond a shadow of a doubt that He alone was the true God. He was the God of Israel.

That has always been the point. Only God could do these types of things. Sure, the devil imitates the things God does, but it is only an imitation. We see that over and over in scripture. The devil manifests his supernatural power and God manifests a supernatural power that is *exponentially* greater. It wasn't that God didn't do the stuff. It was that God's supernatural displays were so off the charts that it caused people to repent and most times in fear and trembling.

How Weird Does it Get?

You can never judge what is of God and what is not by the level of the weirdness. You can't judge by what your comfort level is or by your traditions, or even by what your denomination decides is acceptable. The only criteria for judging what is of God is the Word and the fruit.

Likewise, every good tree bears good fruit, but a bad tree bears bad fruit. A good tree cannot bear bad fruit, and a bad tree cannot bear good fruit. (Matthew 7:17,18)

God is not constrained by us. He is the Boss. He decides, whether we like it or not. He has given us ample precedent in the Word to establish His character so that we can know Him *and* His ways. Therefore we can know what is of Him as well. "Blind faith" is not Biblical faith. We don't blindly believe anything because we have been given a litany of proofs.

His Power Displayed

Someone turns a stick into a snake. Is that demonic or of God? Well, the story told in Exodus chapter seven tells us that God told Moses to cast down his staff and God would turn it into a snake.

The Lord spoke to Moses and Aaron. He said, "Pharaoh will say to you, do a miracle. When he does, speak to Aaron. Tell him, Take your wooden staff and throw it down in front of Pharaoh. It will turn into a snake." (Exodus 7:8,9)

Then of course we know from the same story that Pharaoh's magicians also cast their sticks down and they also became snakes. A similar manifestation but from two different sources. One from God and one from the devil. However Moses' snake ate up the magician's snakes, thereby proving our God's superiority.
How about this? You are fishing with a friend and you accidently drop your fishing pole into the water.

It wouldn't be so bad, but the pole you were using was borrowed. But your friend suddenly tells you "It's OK, I'll just throw this stick into the water and your pole will float to the top."

You would probably think your friend is joking, but if it really happened what would you think then? The power of God or the power of something else? Is your friend even a servant of God? How can you tell, when weird stuff happens?

Now the company of prophets said to Elisha, "As you see, the place where we live under your charge is too small for us. Let us go to the Jordan, and let us collect logs there, one for each of us, and build a place for us to live." He answered, "Do so." Then one of them said, "Please come with your servants." And he answered, "I will." So he went with them. When they came to the Jordan, they cut down trees. But as one was felling a log, his ax head fell into the water. He cried out, "Alas master! It was borrowed!" Then the man of God said, "Where did it fall?" When he showed him the place, he cut off a stick, and threw it in there, and made the iron float. He said ,"Pick it up." So he reached out his hand and took it. (2 Kings 6:1-7)

The key to look at here in this story is not how strange this miracle was, but the fact that "the man of God" was the one who did it. Notice that the scripture *does not say*, "When they saw the man of God do this, they realized he was in deception."

One of my favorite stories from our history is that of Elijah and the prophets of Baal in 1 Kings 18. Elijah goes before the King Ahab and tells him that he has really messed up by serving a different God. Ahab tells him he is a trouble-maker. Elijah arranges a showdown with the false prophets and the show down on Mt. Carmel with the prophets of Baal is a classic example of the supernatural power of the God we know and love on display.

Elijah and the prophets of Baal both build an altar for sacrifice, and Elijah tells them that the God who answers by fire, is the true God. Basically, we will build our altars and the true God will consume the sacrifice by fire.

The prophets of Baal built their altar and then spent the day calling on the name of their god, singing, dancing, cutting themselves with stones, knives and spears but to no avail. He never shows up. Elijah mocks them by telling them that their god is asleep or hard of hearing a or perhaps too busy right now. Then Elijah prepares his sacrifice and has the servants dump so much water on it that the water fills the trenches around the sacrifice.

At the time of sacrifice, the prophet stepped forward and prayed: "Lord, the God of Abraham, Isaac and Israel, let it be known today that you are God in Israel, and that I am your servant and have done all these things at your command. Answer me Lord, answer me, so these people will know that you Lord, are God, and that you are turning their hearts back again." Then the fire of the Lord fell and burned up the sacrifice, the wood, the stones, and the soil, and also licked up the water in the trench. When all the people saw this they fell prostrate and cried, "The Lord-He is God. The Lord-He is God." (1 Kings 18:36-39)

The overwhelming power of God displayed through miracles and supernatural events and encounters is meant to validate God. To show a proof *to cause people to believe, not to lead people astray!*

When Jesus was talking to Phillip in John chapter fourteen about who He is, He told him that even if he believed for no other reason, believe because of the works (miracles) that he had seen Him (Jesus) do.

"Believe me when I say that I am in the Father and the Father is in me, or at least believe on the evidence of the works themselves." (John 14:11)

The sad thing is that with all the miracles, signs and wonders that Jesus did, those with hardened hearts would not believe anyway but rather accused him of manifesting the power of the devil. (Matthew Ch. 12)

This would be a good time to interject a truth about visitations and supernatural encounters. If the fruit of the event or miracle is that people get born again, or healed or delivered from bondage to devils, or that they have a closer walk with Jesus, etc., then chances are it is a manifestation of the true and living God. The Holy Spirit will bear witness of Himself so trust Him. As Jesus pointed out to the Pharisees of His day, if Satan is casting out Satan, he would only be destroying his *own* kingdom.

"And if Satan cast out Satan, he is divided against himself, how shall then his kingdom stand?" (Matthew 12:26)

For the most part, you will not see the devil leading people to salvation, or (truly) healing the sick, or doing anything to exalt the name of Jesus.

An Avalanche of the Supernatural

The entire Bible is chock full of supernatural events from The creation in Genesis to John's Revelation.

Old Testament Examples

*Moses is given leprosy as a sign in Exodus chapter 4.
*The burning bush that was not consumed in Exodus 3.
*Talking animal in Numbers 2, as Balaam's donkey speaks.
*Elijah raises a boy from the dead in 1 Kings 17.
*Jonah swallowed by a giant fish and then spat out to go preach to the people of Nineveh, in Jonah 1.(can you imagine Jonah's appearance after that experience?)
*Joshua stops the sun in Joshua 10.
*Manna sent from Heaven to feed the Tribe of Israel in Exodus 16.
*The walls of Jericho fall down in Joshua 6.

(Archeologists have found that the walls did not fall over, but look as if they had been "pushed" into the ground!)
*Shadrach, Meshach and Abednego walking unscathed in the furnace, not even smelling like smoke in Daniel 3.

New Testament Examples

*The healing of the Centurion's servant in Matthew 8.
*A woman with an issue of blood healed in Mark 5.
*Raising the widow's son from the dead in Luke 7.
*Raising Jairus' daughter from the dead in Mark 5.
*Raising Lazarus from the dead in John 11.
*Jesus walking on the water in John 6.
*Peter walking on the water also.
*The feeding of four-thousand people in Matthew 15.
*Getting the tax money from a fish's mouth in Matthew 17.
*Turning water into wine in John 2.
*An angel appears to Zacharias to tell him that he will have a son in Luke 1.
*The virgin Mary is told by an angel that she will give birth to the savior in Luke 1.
*The Apostles are set free from prison by an angel in Acts 5.
*Peter freed from prison by an angel in Acts 12.
*Paul caught up to Heaven in 2 Corinthians 12
*John, in the Spirit on the Lord's day and giving us the Revelation of Christ. (Book of Revelation)

Early Church History

One thing that we have to give our Catholic brothers credit for is not only the manifestation and promotion of the miraculous from the early church fathers until now, but the fact that the miracles done by those in the Catholic Church have always been so well documented. Every miracle and those who have performed those miracles (by the power of God) are placed in a rigorous review and investigation process that place the supernatural event beyond contestation.

Also, the life of the person who performed the miracle is investigated to determine if their life is in a place where God would indeed use them. Witnesses are gathered, interviews are conducted, medical verification in done, stories are compared and corroborated. Every aspect is looked at to remove any possible natural explanation to the event in question. Those who want to believe that miracles had stopped after the original twelve, have a huge hurdle to leap. God is indeed still with us.

Notable Miracles and Wonders...

*St. Patrick is one of my favorites. St. Patrick is credited with raising over thirty people from the dead. During his life he was known as "the man who raises the dead." Two of the people he raised from the dead were the King's own children. These events are well documented.
*St. Columba is another who raised the dead. He was also well known for his prophetic gifting and would prophesy future events concerning the King and nation. St. Columba also openly and constantly healed the sick, cast out devils and controlled the weather. He also had a close relationship with the angelic host and spoke with angels face to face.
*Move closer to present and we have St. Pio. (Padre Pio) Padre Pio lived a life of the miraculous. It seems that just about everything about him was supernatural. For example, he was known to take very little food for extended periods of time yet still remained robust and healthy. Padre Pio also raised the dead and healed the sick, an example being a woman who brought her deceased baby in her suitcase on a train trip to see the Padre, who then raised the baby up. St. Pio also was well known for bi-location. Many times he would minister to the needs of the people in two different cities at the same time. He also carried the wounds of Christ in his hands for a great part of his life.

To those who are skeptical, let me remind you that God is not bound by our human reasoning or intellect.

Although I have only given a few examples of the miracles and wonders of God, it remains a fact that all through the history of the church, there have been men and women who lived the miraculous as a lifestyle.

In his book, "Saints who Raised the Dead", Father Alfred J. Hebert presents *more than four-hundred documented examples* of men and women who did the "impossible" on a regular basis. Some of whom we all know, and some the average person has never heard of.

The whole point being, as believers we have a supernatural history and heritage, uninterrupted from the creation forward.

If you are a believer you have every right to be excited about what God is doing *now*. You have every right to embrace your birthright and live your faith as a vibrant, exciting adventure and not as a history lesson

God is No Respecter of Persons

Please do not think that you are unqualified or under-qualified to live the kind of lives that these saints lived. If you are a believer, the Bible calls *you* a saint! And from the least to the greatest, God uses the *willing!* If you read the writings of those who lived these extraordinary lives, (St. Pio, St. Teresa of Avila and others) you would know that they encourage us to do the same! They all made it clear that we could and should follow their example and live *our own extraordinary life.*

Then Peter opened his mouth and said, "Of a truth, I perceive that God is no respecter of persons." (Acts 10:34)

Drink Deep

As you read through these stories taken from my life, I encourage you to envision yourself having these things and *greater*. There is no story more compelling or adventure more grand than an authentic supernatural life in God.

God is not boring or dead and He doesn't want our relationship with Him to be those things either. Before you read any further, I would encourage you to pray this prayer with me.

Dear Lord, please forgive my sins. I re-affirm my commitment to you now. I yield myself to You completely. Let Your will be done in my life, my home and in my family, as it is in Heaven. I receive the baptism of the Holy Spirit and fire. I receive your gifts and callings. I receive deliverance from every obstruction of the enemy. I ask You Lord to manifest Your Kingdom in my life more than ever before. Establish Your Kingdom in me and through me. Use me for Your glory. Let the sights and sounds of Heaven be manifest in my life and household. Let me be a Bethel, a Jacobs Ladder and gateway for you Lord. Let my home be a habitation of angels and a place where the Glory of God is tangibly felt. Lord I desire and receive everything that Jesus paid such a high price to provide for me, and I thank You for it. In Christ's name, Amen.

3

THE SOUNDS OF HEAVEN

Probably the most important sound of Heaven is God's voice. The Bible says we are able to hear God's voice and follow Him. Sometimes we hear better than others. Sometimes we follow better than others.

Learning God's Voice

Learning to hear and follow God's voice has definitely been a process for me. Sometimes His voice seems so clear and other times I can't quite discern if it's really His voice or perhaps my own voice I'm hearing. Especially if the voice agrees with my natural inclinations. This first story is just that.

Going to See Randy Clark!

It was Saturday, the eighteenth of April 2010. I had learned that Randy Clark of Global Awakening was going to be Carmi, IL, only four hours away!

I was stoked for the trip and was up early and getting ready. While trying to pick out clothes to wear, I felt that the Lord was telling me to wear my old comfortable jeans. (thank You Jesus!) Now my wife Gordana, would argue that point because she believes I should wear dress clothes when I go to church (because we represent the Lord) but I would always wear jeans if it were up to me. So in obedience to God's voice I put on my comfortable jeans for the trip. Then I had to find a shirt to wear. I pulled out a nice white dress shirt to kind of "dress up" my look a little, when I hear the Lord's voice again telling me to wear my old jean shirt. Ok now I'm thinking that this has got to be me. There's no way God is telling me to wear that ratty old shirt, even though I would really love to. So I wear the white one. I load up my van, everything's a go!

I set out on my journey excited for what God might do. I was praying in the spirit and singing songs and having a great time. I was about at the halfway point when I realized my van was overheating. I had just pulled off the highway so I made it to a gas station. I tried to look under the engine compartment without messing up my nice white shirt but I couldn't see anything. I had to climb underneath and found that there was a nice sized hole in my radiator. I still wanted to try and make it to the meeting, but I realized that if I got stranded four hours away from home I would have to pay a heck of a tow bill. So I bought several gallons of water and some stop leak and set out to make it back home. I had to climb under the van a few times and realized that had I listened to the Lord earlier, I wouldn't have messed up my nice shirt. I stopped many times to get extra water and my two hour drive turned into four or more.

So as I tried to make it home I asked the Lord "*If You can tell me what clothes to wear, why didn't You just tell me not to go?*" The Lord told me it was a training exercise. He said *"The reason you wanted to go see Randy Clark was for an impartation to prepare you for ministry."* Yes, that was true.. The Lord told me *"In ministry, you can't be thrown by stuff like this. This is nothing."*

"Right now you are totally focused on this one small thing. You have to be able to deal with stuff like this <u>and</u> still be ready and aware for the important things, the life and death things."

The Lord continued to talk to me concerning this lesson and then suddenly told me to keep my eyes open. For the next couple minutes I tried to keep aware to see what He was talking about. I came over the rise of a hill and saw a bad accident on the west bound side that I had just been on, only an hour earlier. The Lord told me *"Over there. That's why you're here. I want you to pray."*

So I prayed over the accident and the Lord also told me to continue to pray all the way home. The rest of the drive home from that point, the van did not overheat one time. I didn't have to pull over again and the van made it all the way home.

Did I learn to hear and *obey* God's voice from this? I wish I could tell you *"yes."*

Missionary to Cuba

I know God speaks in dreams. If we really pay attention, I know that we can be led down the right path. Dreams are important. In the middle of July, 2011, I saw the Prophet Bob Jones in a dream. In the dream, Bob told me two very specific things. First, he told me that when I am in places where I am very aware (in the spirit) it means that I have been there many times. Secondly, Bob introduced me to a woman who was a missionary to Cuba and told me to give her two, five dollar bills.

When I awoke from that dream, I didn't think too much about it. It didn't seem like it was relevant to me. After all, my parents had been with a missions organization for several years and I had met missionaries from all over the world but had never met a missionary to or from Cuba. I disregarded the dream.

A few days later, my wife and I found ourselves in Mexico, a gift from our children Matt and Angie for our twenty-fifth anniversary. After arriving, our activities person decided that we needed to go to the luxury resort next door and take a tour. I really didn't want to go but couldn't seem to get out of it. The woman (Cindy) who was giving us the tour was very nice and took us to a wonderful breakfast buffet, and we sat down to chat. Suddenly she starts telling us all about her missionary work to Cuba, and what the Lord was using her for now. I really could have kicked myself because I did not have the two, five dollar bills ready like I had been told to. I explained to her what God had told me, and I gave her a twenty because that was the only size bill I had, but it wasn't the same. I missed it...again. I am still learning.

Go Talk to the Mean Man

This example is a bit more recent, from 2012. Have you ever seen those people, you know, the rough looking ones that you don't really want to mess with? In my work I go to a lot of different businesses and see a lot of people. I happened to be working somewhere one day when I saw a man walk past me . He looked angry and had an expression on his face that said (to me anyway) I don't want to be bothered.

These are the types of people that the Lord always seems to send us to. Suddenly I hear in my spirit, *"Go tell him that I love him and I have a great plan for his life."* Right away I realize this has to be me. No way that this is God talking to me. I ignore the voice and then I hear it again. I start weighing the situation. Mean, angry guy and me telling him *"Jesus loves you."* No it can't be God, but then I heard it again, so this time I didn't even stop to think, because I know if I start to reason I won't obey the word. So I just started walking his way and braced myself. I apologized and then dove in. "Jesus loves you and he has a great plan for your life." He looked at me hard for a second, and then poured out his heart to me. This man who looked angry to me was just in pain. That was the look I was seeing on his face.

We spoke for a while and God was able to meet him and do a work in him. The Lord wanted to love on this man, and He gave me the great honor of carrying the message.

It seems safe to err on the side of grace. If you hear what you think is God's voice telling you to do a good thing, do it. If you're wrong you have still only done a good thing. No harm, no foul.

Voices of Angels

If you have read my previous book, "How to See in the Spirit," You would know that I have had a couple of issues with seeking the gift more than the Giver. (Just a quick heads up. I intend to reveal my mistakes here in this book. You will get all of them in bold print) On this particular night I was on my knees in the living room kneeling in front of the couch and praying with an intensity. It was perhaps two in the morning, no one else up or around and suddenly I heard someone talking to me. ... *In French.*

At this point, although I didn't see anyone I assumed that it was an angel. Although I am reasonably versed in foreign language, I couldn't figure out what he said because I did not know the meaning of the word "coquette." So I got up from my prayer position and went to the computer to look it up. "Flirt." In the context he had used it, it meant flirt. The angel had told me that I was flirting with the Lord.

I wanted the excitement without the commitment. Man! I thought, I have really got to grow up! Anyway, the Lord spoke to me about this for a little while and I got right... again. Thank You Jesus for your patience.

A Lesson in Hearing God

In 2010, my son Matt and I went to the "Light for Dark Days" conference in North Carolina with Gary Oates and Bobby Conner. It was an amazing time of learning and impartation. Plus we had the added benefit of being able to spend a week together enjoying each other's company.

During one of the sessions, Gary Oates was teaching us just how easy it is to hear God's voice. He had us do an exercise where we would close our eyes and imagine ourselves as being part of a Bible story where the Lord was involved and ask the Lord a question. Matt had an amazing experience because of this exercise and I also heard from the Lord. I had asked Him about His plans for my life, and He told me, *"I have great plans for you but you have to be obedient."* I won't go into more detail on that one, but I did hear clearly from the Lord. We had a really great time there, and met wonderful people from all over.

When we got home, My wife Gordana and my daughter Angie naturally wanted to hear all about our trip. We talked about the trip, telling them all the wonderful things and we also told them about the exercise in hearing God's voice. (we didn't tell them what God had told us personally) I told my daughter Angie *"try it, just pick out a Bible story, close your eyes and ask the Lord a question"*. She was hesitant and said she didn't know what to ask. I told her *"Just ask the Lord if He has a word for me then."* So she closed her eyes and was still for a couple of minutes, then said *"I don't know about this."* I said *"What, just tell us."* She hesitated, then said, *"He says He wants you to obey."* The fact that the Lord spoke to my daughter so clearly and plainly, really showed me the validity of what Gary Oates had taught us.

If you do this every day with a notebook handy to write everything down that the Lord says, you will find your ear inclined to His voice. He will make it easy to hear Him.

The Breath of God

In 2012, my wife Gordana and I attended a prophetic conference in Ohio. During worship suddenly a strange and wonderful sound rang out, it was the sound of a shofar! Gordana fell in love with that sound and decided that she had to have one. The girl there at the meeting who had the shofar (she also had a sword, how cool is that!) gave Gordana the name and address of the man she had gotten it from. So it wasn't long after that, that we found ourselves on a road trip from Carmel, Indiana to Fairfield, Ohio, to see Dennis McKirahan, the founder and director of Shofar Call International. It was an amazing day! Brother Dennis spent an incredible amount of time with us, teaching us and praying over us and anointing us, then sending us away with the perfect shofar for Gordana. This trip was not just about "buying a shofar" but far more.

When we got home and our family all got together in the evening to read the Bible and pray, we capped off the evening by blowing the shofar. We all took turns trying to blow the shofar and make it sound the way it's supposed to. Our son Matt seemed to have a natural gift for it and the sound he produced rang out loud and clear for a long time. It was a really wonderful experience.

But soon, Matt had to leave for work and the rest of us were just kind of relaxing before bed. About three minutes after Matt left, he called to tell us "I was driving away from the house and suddenly I saw three orbs of light fall from the sky into our neighborhood!" He knew that they were angels and we did too. Do you think Matt's testimony caused us to blow the shofar all the more? Of course it did!

We then proceeded over the next couple of weeks to blow the shofar throughout the house, in every room, closet, nook and cranny. I wasn't aware of just how powerful this was until a couple of weeks later.

Overwhelming Angelic Response

Many times before we go to bed at night, we blow the shofar to set the spiritual atmosphere in the house. It seemed to bring a peace and presence that was tangible. It had been perhaps a month or so after we had brought the shofar home, when the following occurred.

We had blown the shofar several times in our bedroom and then went to bed. My wife Gordana sometimes (many times) is in intercession about bedtime and this day was no exception so I went downstairs to pray. I sat down in my "prayer chair" (a large comfortable chair in our living room) I prayed for a while and at some point I fell asleep. When I woke up, I woke up in the spirit realm. That is, when I awoke my spiritual eyes were wide open. I looked around me and saw perhaps fifty angels all standing around in groups, talking to each other. I was in awe. I was drawn to two very big angels who were standing just to my right, talking to each other. They looked like very powerful warriors and they were dressed in similar attire but one had blond hair and one had dark hair, about shoulder length.

I don't know what they thought about me, because when I saw them I went over to them and just kind of stood there gawking at them. (In my own defense, they presented a pretty awesome appearance) They continued their conversation unfazed. I recognized the angel with the dark hair as one who had spoken to me once before about a year or so earlier. He was easy to remember because he reminded me of Mel Gibson from the movie "Braveheart."

This encounter really made me aware of the power that the shofar holds. It isn't just a symbolic thing but a powerful sound in the Kingdom Realm. You should probably get one.

Strange Noises in the House

The way I was raised, any supernatural occurrence including sounds would automatically be assumed to be demonic in nature. Because in many churches the belief is "all supernatural is of the devil." So even though I really knew better, I found myself thinking that way at times. The big problem with this is that it conflicts with the kind of prayer that I pray over my household. In the course of my prayers I will at some point say,

"Lord let your angels manifest their presence and power openly in our lives and in our home, to bless us and encourage us."

When the Lord answers a prayer like that, anything can happen.

Every time a Bell Rings...

I know what you're thinking. Mike has really lost it. Now he's giving us angelology from "It's a Wonderful Life." Well not exactly. I have a habit of praying the prayer I just mentioned above, a lot. Why? Because I want the atmosphere of Heaven in my home and in my family. The angels carry an incredible amount of God's glory on them. So much so that if they did not veil it from us sometimes, we wouldn't be able to handle it. (more on that later) I want that in my home.

We have a decorative bell hanging on our back door. On many occasions, we have been in the basement watching television or videos when we hear the bell ring. I will be honest with you. When that first started to happen, I rebuked and prayed and carried on so it would stop. After a couple of times of doing that, I heard an angel speak to my thoughts. He said, *"You can't have it both ways. Either you want us to manifest our presence openly, or you don't. Pick one."* So now when we hear the bell, We just say *"Thanks for being on the job."*

Footsteps

A lot of the experiences I've had in God have been after hearing some wonderful testimony about what god is doing in someone else's life. It's the power of the testimony. (Bill Johnson of Bethel Church teaches on this)
I heard a really cool testimony from Steven Brooks of Steven Brooks International. In his life and ministry the angels are really hands on, if you know what I mean. Those of you familiar with Steven Brooks will know exactly what I'm talking about.

I once heard Brother Steven talking about one of the angels that works with him. This angel will wake him up at night to pray, and grab him by the hand to help him up. Pretty cool right? That's what I thought too. The more I thought about it, the more I wanted that experience as well. God is no respecter of persons, right? So, one night as I lay in bed trying to decide if I would get up to pray for a while, I got the idea to put the decision in the hands of the angels. I lifted my hand up in the air and said *"Angel of the Lord, you know that Steven Brooks' angels help him out of bed to pray. If I'm supposed to pray, take my hand and help me up."* I stayed like that with my hand in the air for well over a minute. Suddenly, I heard one of the kids trying to sneak up the stairs. I got up and crept over to the stairway to surprise whoever it was but the surprise was on me. There was no one there! I bet that angel had a good laugh! I can almost picture him saying *"So, you won't get up huh?"* Well I thought that was pretty smart so I stayed up to pray anyway. (Which I should have done in the first place)

Sometimes I am amazed when I look back over some of the foolish things I have said and done concerning the Lord and the Heavenly Host. I don't mean any disrespect, but it sure comes out that way sometimes. I know that God is very merciful and I sure am glad for that.

Fearless Confidence

We don't have to be in fear over any noise, movement or manifestation. Even if something does turn out to be the enemy, you still don't have to be in fear because we have authority and the promise of our Lord.

"Behold I give unto you authority to tread on serpents and scorpions, and over all the power of the enemy, and nothing shall by any means hurt you." (Luke 10:19)

We embrace the angels, and we drive out the devils.

Clearly Hearing The Sound Of God's Voice

A couple of years ago I spoke to an intercessor for one of the ministries who have helped me in my own journey. The woman clearly heard God's voice. It wasn't by accident either. I mentioned in my last book about times of pressing into God that went beyond the "norm". This intercessor took it up a notch.

She had told me that she felt God telling her to lock herself away for a season and pray. So she called all of her family and told them that she wouldn't be available for a while. She spent I believe twelve weeks in prayer before she came back out into the world. She told me that she had so much revelatory knowledge that it scared her. She knew things about everyone. She knew intimate details of people's lives... what car their boss drove, how many children and what their names were, all kinds of stuff.

When you tell people that God knows all about them and He's revealing this because He loves them and wants a relationship with them, it's a compelling reason to believe. She led a lot of people to Christ through these words of knowledge.

We can't all lock ourselves away for a month or three, but we can seek God more and believe Him to use us in this way also.

4

THE BLESSINGS OF GOD

"Bring ye all the tithes into the storehouse, that there may be meat in mine house, and prove me herewith, saith the LORD of hosts, if I will not open you the windows of Heaven, and pour you out a blessing , that there shall not be room enough to receive it." (Malachi 3:10)

God's promises of provision are so awesome. God is not a man that he should lie, so take hold of *every* promise and declare them over your life, family and circumstances.

We hear it said so much that it almost sounds cliché, but it is true, you can't out give God. There are many of you that just read that and cannot relate. You have done this (sown) and not seen an increase that is so great that there is not room enough to receive it. You believe it and you want to believe it but there is a disconnect somewhere. Our family faced these same issues and I pray that the following testimonies of God's supernatural provision help you and encourage you.

Confirmations

One of the best things that the Lord has shown us is that He is willing not only to tell us expressly where to sow seed, but He will also confirm it. In the past, we had a bad habit of listening to a message, hearing about the special blessing of a debt free house, the favor of God and other things, and we would sow because *we wanted* that blessing! That is the blessing we were looking for. Is it wrong to desire those blessings? No, it's not. But we were not consulting the Lord in a serious way as to where *He* wanted the seed to go.

Now, when my wife and I feel moved by the Lord to give, I will ask her or she will ask me, *"How much did the Lord tell you to give?"* and very often it will be the same amount. The Lord will confirm it. If you give that way, you may be putting your seed to work where God tells you and not following your natural compassion or desire for a blessing promised of man.

One day my wife Gordana and I were taking a prayer walk around the neighborhood and she turned to me and said *"I feel we are supposed to give some money to so and so."* I told her that I felt the same, and an amount came into my mind. It was a rather large amount and I knew that if this was of God she would also hear this same amount. She told me the amount that God told her and it matched exactly. The word was confirmed and we put His money where He told us to.

Another time Gordana was on the phone talking to somebody and I was there listening to her side of it. During the conversation, although the person didn't mention it, she felt that we were supposed to give money to the person that she was talking to. I didn't ask the Lord but He spoke to me anyway and told me (in my heart) that we were to give $285.00 to fix this person's car. Later in the conversation it came out that this person's car was indeed in need of repair and the estimate was $250.00. Did the Lord get the amount wrong? No, the estimate was off by $35.00.

Hear God For Yourself

My point is this, if you learn to listen for and hear God's voice you will learn to sow where you are supposed to. *You will sow where your blessing lies.*

What about all the times that people prophesy an increase if you obey and plant the special seed? Is that of God or not? Here again *you* have to hear His voice even in this! It could very well be a word from God given to a man or woman of God for three hundred very specific people, but you may not be one of them. I have heard it said that *"delay is disobedience."* That is absolutely true if you have heard from **God**. If you have not heard clearly from God, then delay is *wisdom*. You take it before the Lord and ask Him to confirm if this is indeed something from Him for you or not. If you don't hear yes, save your money and sow it elsewhere.

We are stewards of the provision God gives us and *we are accountable* for it. So learn to hear and discern God's voice.

On My Soapbox

Yes, I am on the soapbox because this is important if you want to experience the miracles of provision I am about to share with you. If you come across someone and feel God wants you to give this person fifty dollars for groceries but you don't have it because you pitched your last fifty in the plate, *only* because it was a good cause, you are missing God's best.

God Gives Seed to the Sower

Make a commitment to God that you will be a sower. I mean really do it. And fulfill it. Show God that you are trustworthy in small things and He will increase you. Tell Him He doesn't own ten percent, but one-hundred percent and that you will follow His voice.

My Old Truck

I had purchased an old truck that I thought I would clean up and resell to make a few bucks. I paid a thousand dollars for it and hoped to make several hundred more, but months had past and no one had even stopped by to look at the truck. One day I was outside standing in the driveway looking at the truck and the Lord spoke to me. " *I want you to give Randy* (not his real name) *a thousand dollars."* I told the Lord that I would be glad to but I don't have a thousand dollars. He then asked me if I still wanted to sell my truck and I said *"Yes."* I listened to hear anything further but that was it. So I just continued on with the chores I had been doing.

That same night I fell into a dream. In the dream, I was standing in our bedroom upstairs and looking out the window at my truck sitting in the driveway. I saw two men walking around the truck and examining it. One of the men was white with dark hair, and one of the men appeared to be Hispanic. I could even hear what they were saying. The Hispanic man was saying *"We can build wooden sides on the bed to hold mulch."* In the dream the white man with dark hair handed me twenty-six hundred dollars. It was a very real dream and I felt it was significant.

Two days later on a Saturday, I walked outside to do yard work and I saw the same two men from the dream, and they were looking at the truck. They asked me some questions about the truck, started it up and listened to it run, then paid me, you guessed it, twenty-six hundred dollars for it. The Lord not only gave me back the money for the truck but also gave me a thousand to bless Randy, and a very nice eight hundred dollars for myself! God gives seed to the sower! The Bible tells us that He gives seed to the sower but I'm not sure if we have a complete revelation of that. If He tells you to sow He will provide the seed. Simple as that.

More Confirmations and More Seed

In my book "How to See in the Spirit", I talk about the prophecy that Apostle Art McGuire of Joshua Ministries spoke over me concerning the writing of the book . Now let me tell you the rest of the story.

After the Apostle prophesied that I was to write the book, I was at work one day mulling it over in my mind. I asked the Lord to please give me a confirmation that this was indeed from Him. Very often the Lord will give me a scripture (a scripture reference will pop up in my thoughts) that is spot on about whatever situation I am praying about.

It's really funny but sometimes I find myself having conversations with the Lord and it all seems so natural and normal and flowing. This was one of those times. I had asked the Lord to give me a confirmation and suddenly I heard, *"I will give you a confirmation. I will give you a thousand dollars, how's that for a confirmation?"* I had been through this kind of thing often enough at this point not to speak out in unbelief. I simply said *"Thank You."*

The Lord continued to talk to me. *"You can keep it all and use it however you would like."* I said *"Thank You."* The Lord then said, *"Would you be willing to sow a portion of it? You don't have to if you don't want to , but would you be willing to?"* I said *"What do You want me to do?"* Then the Lord said *"Sow, so I can give you the greater blessing."* I said *"OK."*

So the Lord gave me the money and asked me to sow some of it. Notice I said He *gave* me the money. I didn't have the money in my hand but His word is rock solid. He will *never* lie to you so if He says it, it's done. Also notice (again) that He gives seed to the sower. He could have given me a scripture but gave me seed instead and more!

Two days later, my wife and I were relaxing in the kitchen with a cup of coffee when there was a knock at the door. A couple that we hadn't seen in about six months just happened to show up. We had a nice fellowship and after a while the man took me aside and slipped me an envelope. In the envelope was ten, one hundred dollar bills. God indeed gives seed to the sower.

Learn to hear His voice on this subject. Here is something I do on a regular basis. If I feel a nudge to bless someone, I will tell the Lord *"All The money that you give me supernaturally today (or this week) I will give to this person."* Again I will remind you that God has promised to give you seed.

You may be tested if you do this. God will put money in your hand to train you to be faithful. He won't make it difficult to obey Him but He may test your faith. If you make this kind of promise with ten dollars in your mind and God puts a hundred or a thousand in your hand, what will you do? He has given you a real opportunity to grow your faith. Go for it!

Bless Dennis

I had made a new friend about a month earlier and one day as I went about my business, I heard the Lord speak. *"I want to bless Dennis."* I told the Lord that whatever He gave me supernaturally, I would know that it was for Dennis. The next day, I was given one hundred and fifty dollars. I knew it was God's money and He was entrusting it to me to give it to Dennis. So I did. It's that easy.

Do not struggle and beat yourself up about your money. Where should we put it and who should we bless? Let God lead you. He is a good Father and he will teach you His ways. Do not get bound in some legalistic condemnation over this part of your Christian life.

The Godfather

Andrew Wommack teaches on this very topic. He says that many people are taught that if they don't give the right tithe amount in the right place, God will take it from them through medical bills or unforeseen expenses. He says that that kind of behavior is more like the Godfather than God the Father! Would you punish your children for trying to obey you but not getting it exactly right. I sure hope not.

Believing for the Outrageous

I almost left this testimony out. Then it occurred to me that this would be a chance to brag on how great the Lord is and encourage someone in a similar situation.

About twelve years ago, our family found ourselves in the position where we needed to move. The school fees that we were paying for the kids were astronomical and we just couldn't continue. So we began a search for a new home. For some unknown reason, I felt that we should believe for a "dream home". On a repair tech's salary, we really couldn't afford a dream home, but I felt we should look for one anyway.

I really went way beyond reason on this. I asked my wife Gordana and the kids what were the things that they would like in our new home. I was serious about this and made a list. We wrote down every feature that we would like to have and that would be the house we would look for. It was about a dozen things. It was a crazy list by all normal standards. I searched diligently for this very house for two years. I looked on every side of town in almost every neighborhood. The only place I did not look was a north side city that had a reputation as being a very affluent. My thinking was that I might be able to find our dream house in the right neighborhood but there was no way that I could afford it in this north side city. Silly me. I was putting a limit on God.

After two years of searching, driving around Indianapolis every weekend looking at houses, I was starting to get weary of it. On this particular weekend I again got on the realtor sites on the computer and put in my search criteria. On a fluke, just for the heck of it, I entered in the name of that city I knew we could never afford. I found a house that appeared to fit part of the criteria. The house was two story, four bedrooms and three baths. The price looked too good to be true. It was probably a typo but I decided to go check it out.

When I pulled up to the house I could not believe my eyes. Although this house was completely overgrown with weeds and ground cover from two years of sitting empty, it had every feature from our list. *Every feature.* I want you to notice that I said the house was empty for two years. For two years I had refused to look in this city because of my natural reasoning. I believe God held it for us. I immediately went to the realtor and made a full price offer(without consulting my wife) because that's how sure I was that this was the place. Within two hours they accepted my offer. What I did not know, was that the house had only been put on the market hours before I "found" it.

And immediately after my offer had been accepted, the listing agent had almost twenty people come forward wanting to purchase the house. Talk about God's supernatural timing!

We have now lived in this house for more than ten years. The neighborhood is quiet and very nice. On Sunday mornings we can hear the church bells ring all throughout the neighborhood. The neighbors are all very nice people. It has been a real blessing from God.

In the natural it was impossible. God *made* it possible. God really desires great things for us and this taught me that we have to tell Him our dreams and believe that He will bring them to pass. He wants us happy!

Supernatural Multiplication

This miracle is not near the biggest financial miracle I have witnessed, but it is definitely among the strangest. Our family and Gordana's friend Kim had gone to Ohio to attend a prophetic conference with Heidi Baker of Iris Ministries of Mozambique. After one of the sessions, we decided to run through the McDonalds drive thru and get something quick to eat. After we ordered and pulled forward, Kim who was driving was going to pay. My wife Gordana gave her six dollars and I gave her three. She suddenly said *"this is way too much money, I don't need this much."* So Kim gave back to Gordana her six dollars. Then Kim said it was still too much and gave me back my three dollars. Still leaving her with enough money to pay for all the food. The money had multiplied enough to pay for all the food and give us all of our money back. That one kept us up half the night talking about God's miraculous power!

All Over The World

These types of miracles are happening all over the world. Iris Ministries of Mozambique, are experiencing this type of miracle on an ongoing basis as well as David Hogan's ministry in Mexico. Not only with money and things, but food as well, just like the Bible days!

Decree! Don't Let the devil Steal From You!

I am including this supernatural event in this section on blessings because it ties our ability or privilege to decree things that affect our financial blessings and provisions to the outcome we expect and desire and *need*.

Gate Key and Time Card

At the company where I work, we have an automated security gate that requires a keycard. We also have a time clock that requires we "clock in" with a time card that we are issued. These are two things that I have normally kept together in a safe place, due to their importance. After work each day when I get home, I unload my pockets into my desk drawer. I lay my cards along with my keys in the drawer.

One morning after getting ready for work, I went to my desk and began loading up all of my stuff. My keys, my wallet and pens, loose change etc.. However, I could not find my cards anywhere. I asked if anyone had been in the drawer, but no one had. I then proceeded to search throughout the house but to no avail. I knew however, that I had put those cards in the desk drawer. So over the course of about thirty minutes, I came back to that drawer three times to take everything out and go through it. Nothing. I began to get aggravated and suddenly a story popped into my mind of Bobby Conner talking about decreeing the return of a pocket knife that Bob Jones had given him, that had been stolen from his hotel room. Bobby had already gone on to another city but he still demanded that his knife be returned, "I want my knife back!" is what he exclaimed. Out of "nowhere" his knife dropped onto his bed.

God is no respecter of persons, so I shouted "I want my cards back!" I immediately got the sense that I should go again to the drawer, and there, laying right on top of everything in plain view were my time card and gate key. I believe there was a greater significance to this lesson. One, the power of a testimony. I have seen this over and over in my own life. When I hear a wonderful testimony from someone, I apply it to my own life if I can and God always does something. And two, that the devil will steal our access if he can (gate key) and our time/ finances. (time card)

We have been given the power and authority as believers of decreeing a thing so that it might come to pass. In these days we must do this!

"You will also decree a thing, and it will be established for you: and light will shine on your ways. (Job 22:28)

The Value of a Penny

I have a penny that I keep in a blue velvet lined jewel box. The penny holds no value to the world but is priceless to me.

One evening my wife Gordana and I were relaxing and watching television together. It may have been House Hunters International, because that was one show we watched together. Gordana, who probably works harder and more diligently than just about anyone I know, began to talk about being tired and wanting a vacation and wouldn't it be nice if we could get away, etc..

I have to be honest, many times I have thought "I am tired too." And "I would like to have a break too." But for some reason (The Lord) I was overcome with compassion. I put my arms around her and began to pray over her and bless her and ask God to give her strength and refreshing. I asked Him to supernaturally give her a vacation and bring His joy upon her. I probably prayed over her for five minutes or so, just really and sincerely blessing her.

As I held her, my arms were around her and my hands were in loose fists. They were closed, but not tightly. All of the sudden, I felt something drop into my hand. I felt something drop into my *closed* hand. I pulled back from her and opened my hand, and there lay a shiny penny! I was dumbfounded. In my usual manner (unfortunately) I began looking for natural, logical reasons as to how a penny could fall into my closed hand. Many scenarios passed through my mind but none were plausible. Only the miraculous made sense.

But why? Why would God drop a penny into my hand? I pondered this for quite awhile, but came up with nothing. Then I decided to get on the internet and type in "a penny drops." I soon found out what the Lord was trying to tell me. You see, the meaning of a penny drops, is "a sudden understanding" or "a revelation."

After learning this, I realized that the Lord was telling me that when I began to have compassion and pray from that place of love and compassion, I was finally "getting it."

It was a confirmation from Heaven that this is what God desires from us. That we might have compassion and show His love. That is what the life of a believer is supposed to be about and I had finally started to get a glimpse of that. And...a penny dropped.

From Decree to Complain

I could probably relay this next story in a way that makes me look better, but it would not show the complete reality of God's goodness. So here goes.

One day last year I was just starting my work day, when I received a semi-frantic call from my daughter Angie."*Dad, I'm downtown at school and was walking to class when I realized that I don't have my car keys. I must have dropped them somewhere.*" After talking to Angie for a few minutes we determined that she had not left them in the car, didn't have them on her or in her purse and didn't have a clue where she could have dropped them. In my mind, I was trying to figure it out and came up with the idea that I was going to have to call a locksmith to deal with this.

As I was pondering the situation, a testimony from Pau Keith Davis came to mind. In this testimony, he was talking about having taken in a young girl who had been involved in witchcraft, to help her get her life together.

He relayed that once they had all went out to eat and had accidently left the keys locked in the car. They also had talked about calling a locksmith, but the young girl said "Why? You don't have to do that." And she proceeded to lay her hand over the lock area and the lock popped open. Of course they explained to her that she was not to do stuff like that anymore, but the point is that she did it.

I complained *"Lord it is not fair that someone operating in that spirit would be able to do that but I who also need similar help, operating in your power can't. An angel should find those keys for her."* The Lord told me to call Angie back and tell her to look in her pockets again. So I did, but Angie said *"Dad, I have looked in all my pockets several times and besides that, I know I didn't put them in my pockets. I was carrying them on top of my books."*

Angie called me back about two minutes later. She had found the keys in a fake pocket on her coat that she had never used. That's the mercy of God, and the power of testimony! I am not suggesting that anyone start complaining as a method of prayer however. I seem to remember a Bible story about a bunch of snakes biting complainers. (Numbers 21:5)

Supernatural provision is an inheritance for those who love and obey God. Believe it!

5

LET THERE BE LIGHT

And this is the message which we have heard from Him and now are reporting to you: God is light, and there is no darkness in Him at all. (1 John 1:5)

For you were formerly darkness, but now you are light in the Lord; walk as children of light. (Ephesians 5:8)

Over the course of the last several years, the Lord has been opening our spiritual eyes to experience many strange and wonderful sights. Among these are supernatural displays of light. Because these types of manifestations make no natural sense, most people dismiss everything they might see as "tricks of the light' or "their eyes playing tricks on them". They are neither. If you pay attention to these things as you experience them, they open up and increase. They also become more visible. I would encourage you to keep this in mind as God breaks this open in your life. The following stories contain many of those manifestations.

Diamonds Hanging in Mid Air

On the fifteenth of April, 2010, I had been sent to a client location to repair some equipment there. After having done the work, I then went to see the company contact person and let her know that the work had been completed.

As I stood in her office waiting for her to finish her phone call so that I could talk to her. I absentmindedly glanced around her office just to occupy myself. Suddenly about four feet in front of me and two feet to the right, I saw a prism of light of sorts hanging in mid-air. It hung in mid–air for about two seconds and then was gone. At least according to my journal and my recollection that's what occurred. Having a bit more understanding now, I would say that whatever or whoever I was seeing was actually still there, I just could not see them.

To describe this light very accurately, I would say it looked like a diamond encrusted belt or belt buckle about a foot and a half wide. The way it appeared was as if someone was wearing this and happened to turn so the reflection of it became apparent to me.

I asked the Lord if I should share this with the contact but was not led to do so.

The Lightnings of God?

Wednesday evening I was in the basement thanking the Lord for all He has done and all He is doing. I happened to look up and saw a spark jump in mid-air about three feet over my head. It was a bluish color about six to eight inches long. Just a sudden FLASH... then it was gone.

The Lightnings of God!

This was one of the most spectacular displays I have ever seen in the natural realm. On this particular day I had gotten home from work and my wife Gordana told me that she had seen some strange greenish light outside but close to our house, as she stood at the sink looking out the window. I didn't think too much about it because I hadn't seen it. I wasn't sure from her description if this was something natural or supernatural.

She had brought it up several more times early in the evening, so I knew it must have been something significant but still had no frame of reference.

Later in the evening, we were in the basement watching television when with no warning two bolts of lightning, one immediately following the other flashed through our basement. They entered through the south wall of the basement and exited through the north wall. We looked at each other stunned. We both had a sense that they were angels, but had no idea why they were there or what they were doing. We talked about it for a long time and of course we also thanked the Lord and worshipped Him for His almighty power, and for giving His angels charge over us. Then after awhile, we kind of went on about our business.

Two hours later we were upstairs and all getting ready for bed. Angie, our daughter and I were in my bedroom just kind of talking about the Lord and the great things He was doing, and Gordana was in our son Matt's room doing something. All of the sudden I saw the lightning again! Two bolts, one right after the other came in through the south end of the bedroom wall and then went out the north end. I ran into the hallway and met my wife who had also run into the hallway. "Did you see that!" we both exclaimed. What appeared to be physical lightning shooting through our house twice, and once outside as well gave us a lot to think about and pray about. It still blesses me to even think about it now.

Orbs of Light

I don't recall and I didn't make note of the first orbs of light we began to see. Like many people, we dismissed this supernatural manifestation as natural tricks of the light, etc.. After a while, you realize they are not natural when the "coincidences" occur over and over. Orbs of all sizes and colors appearing everywhere makes it very difficult to dismiss them.

Ash Wednesday at Mount Carmel

On February twenty second of 2012, Gordana and I went on a prayer walk around our neighborhood, The Village of Mount Carmel. It was a beautiful day and a wonderful walk and prayer time for us. Towards the end of our walk we passed by Our Lady of Mount Carmel Church, only a couple of blocks from our home. When we were directly in front of the church, my eyes were opened and I saw *at the very least,* hundreds of orbs of light filling the sky over the church.

The orbs all appeared to be close to the same size, and were all mostly of a pale orange to pinkish color. I was able to see this sight for a good thirty seconds, until we were well away from the church.

Orbs in Traffic

I mentioned some of these occasions in my book How to See in the Spirit, but they bear repeating here because I believe them to be encouraging to those who are seeking such things.

One morning I was in traffic not far from my home and noticed a ball of light, peach colored, above a car in front of me. This orb of light was very close to being over top of the woman driving.

Once, on my way home from work, I pulled up to a stoplight and just happened to look above the traffic light. (I say just happened to...but I continually look around for the things unseen) There was a faint glow of blue up in the sky above the lights. I had thought to dismiss it, but since I was stopped anyway, I decided just to pay attention for a few seconds and see what happened.

As I focused on this faint glow, it grew in intensity and substance to the point where it almost looked like a solid ball hanging in the air. Had I moved on, I wouldn't have seen it.

I want to take a second to mention that for those of you seeking such things, the spiritual sight and visitations of angels etc., acknowledgement of small things is very important. The small things like orbs of light or flashes of light or movement in the atmosphere are important gateways. As you honor the little things, God will give you increase. You will begin to have greater experiences and manifestations of His Kingdom around you.

Huge Ball of Light

One day I was stopped at another traffic light, when I looked up just in time to see a huge orb of light, golden yellow in color, kind of like a sun actually, floating across the intersection seemingly on its own with no vehicle or person nearby.

Don't Scare the Dog!

One evening my wife Gordana, who is an intercessor, was beginning to engage with the angels who show up to help her. I have asked them (the angels) several times to allow me a clear vision of them, but the only thing I get is veiled movement of white light that appears around her and in the room in general.

On this particular day I told the angels "Come on! Give me a break, I'm her husband! Give me something!" Immediately after saying this to them, a brilliant flash of blue light filled the room startling me and causing our little shih tzu, Meche (little bear) to jump from the foot of the bed and bury his face under my arm for protection! It was pretty cool, but they still have not revealed their faces to me.

Engulfed in Flames

This particular testimony really reveals just how powerful your prayers really are. That maybe when we pray, our prayers are more literally manifested than we realize.

One Saturday morning I was awake but still laying in bed, talking to my wife who was already up getting ready for work. I closed my eyes because I figured I can talk to her just as easy with my eyes closed, but when I did I saw that the entire room was engulfed in flames. The entire room was aflame! I opened my eyes and I could no longer see the flames. I closed my eyes again, and once again I could see fire on all the walls and climbing up on the ceiling. When I opened my eyes again I could no longer see them and when I closed my eyes again I couldn't see them any longer. What a way to start the day! I was stoked!

After seeing Gordana off to work, I sat down in my prayer chair to pray and worship and wait on the Lord. The event that the Lord had shown me inspired me. At about ten in the morning, I was still in my chair when I received a phone call from a friend of mine. The first thing he said to me was *"Guess what I've been doing?"* I told him I had no idea. He said, *"I have spent the entire night praying the fire of God upon your family!"*

When he said that, I received a revelation that the prayers we pray are more powerful than we realize and the Lord opened my eyes to see the reality of this.

You Can "See the Light"

The shifts of light in the spirit realm are more evident and available than most realize. I see them every day that I choose to and so can you. If you spend a few minutes looking every day during the twilight hours, just before going to sleep or immediately upon waking, you will see more easily things in the realm of the spirit.

As you relax and look around you before you begin moving about, you will see subtle lights and colors and movements. The more you focus on these things, the more they will manifest around you. They will become more evident to you.

Desire for spiritual things is a key. If you seek you will find.

Ask, and it shall be given you; seek, and ye shall find; knock, and it shall be opened unto you. (Matthew 7:7)

6

ANGELS APPEARING AS MEN

Although I now believe that I have probably seen many, many angels appearing as men without realizing it , my first encounter that I had conscious knowledge of is the following.

Rebuked by an Angel

On this day, I had gone grocery shopping with my wife and mother in law. As we were walking across the parking lot towards the entrance of the grocery store , a woman on a cell phone pulled into the parking lot seemingly narrowly missing an elderly woman walking. When the woman on the cell phone got out of her car, she was still in conversation oblivious to what had just happened.

I tried to dismiss it and move on, but couldn't seem to do it. I mulled it over and over in my mind, "How rude of her", "She needs to know about this" etc.. After about ten minutes of entertaining these thoughts, I went and found the woman in the store. She was still involved in conversation as she shopped and I approached her.

As I approached her, I noticed a rather large man standing to my left with an empty shopping cart, just looking at me. For some reason I said to myself, "*I think he is a priest.*" I walked past the man and approached the woman. I began telling her about what she had done, how she had almost run over the old woman and that she needed to be more careful and aware. The woman disagreed and argued with me and said it never happened which made me even angrier.

As I continued to talk to the woman, the "man" pushed his cart in between the woman and I and looked at me and said "*You need to walk away.*" I ignored him basically and continued to argue with the woman. He again said "*You need to walk away.*" I still argued with the woman. The third time he told me to walk away, I took a step toward him and felt something that made me shake violently. I stepped back from him and the shaking stopped. I then realized that even though the man was quite large and had pushed his cart between us, the woman had never even looked at him. Even though he had spoken telling me to walk away, the woman never acknowledged him at all.

It all came in an instant. Revelation, that is. I knew then that he was an angel and I had better do what he is telling me to do. I felt repentant. I was sorry I had spoken to the woman in such a manner. I apologized over and over. I kept muttering "*I'm so sorry, I'm so sorry.*"

As the woman walked away and the man began to walk away, I *thought* to myself ,"*That is not like me at all. Why did I do that.*" The man suddenly turned and answered my thought. He said " *She didn't answer you the way you thought she should.*" Then he walked behind the magazine rack and I turned my head for an instant and he was gone. I went around the corner to see if maybe he was still there, bent over or hiding or some other natural explanation, but of course he was gone. I felt the fear of the Lord on me as I realized that I had ignored his instruction three times. I realized that I need to be more aware and more loving.

Angel Over the Mall

My wife Gordana used to work at a shopping mall about twenty minutes from our house. One day I borrowed her car to use for the day. I figured that I would just pick her up at the end of her day. The only variable was, if my wife had more clients or customers show up even after I got to the mall, I would either have to wait for her or leave and make a return trip.

So of course *this* day was one of *those* days. I had actually gotten to the mall about a half hour early and then when I got there I found out that my wife had just committed herself to two more hours of work. So I was looking at a two and a half hour wait. I didn't really want to drive home and waste the time or the gas. I didn't really want to hang out in the mall for two and a half hours. You can only cruise the food court for free samples so many times before they start looking at you funny. What to do?

I suddenly got a brilliant idea! Why don't I do a prayer walk around the mall! That would kill a lot of time and I would actually be doing something useful, changing the spiritual atmosphere. So I set out on my prayer walk. I walked around the interior of the mall praying out loud in tongues, walking sometimes into stores and sometimes not. I *sang* in tongues a lot because it's a way of praying that makes you look like less of a nut. People sing right? Well after one lap I still had loads of time so I did another lap. After the second lap, I still had a lot of time so I decided to move my prayer walk to the outside of the building. I then walked around a large portion of the outside of the mall. I didn't realize until I began walking that it would be considerably more walking! But I had committed myself. I walked around the mall and made it back to the main entrance, a little tired but spiritually refreshed to be honest.

I still had about twenty minutes of free time so I headed to the food court. I figured I could use the facilities and also get a little nourishment. After using the facilities and washing my hands, I walked out into the food court portion of the mall.

As I walked into the food court, a handsome young black man in his mid thirties approached me. He smiled and held out his hand and shook mine and said *"I want you to know that I appreciate your being here today."* I was a little confused. Revelation was not instant but there was something about the way he spoke that carried something more. Then he spoke again, but this time to my mind and all confusion was immediately cleared up. He said "I am the angel over this mall." Then he turned and walked away.

I was so glad I listened to the Lord's voice and did the prayer walk! I will be honest and tell you that I have since done many more prayer walks at the mall, but have not seen him again. But I know he sees me! And more importantly the Lord sees!

Harold the Angel

The Lord tests our hearts. If you haven't thought too much about entertaining angels unaware, you need to.

Be not forgetful to entertain strangers: for thereby some have entertained angels unawares. (Hebrews 13:2)

One of the churches that we attend is situated in a neighborhood that is impoverished. There are many times when people show up in the church basement after church for only the fellowship hour because there is food always provided. Just like in any church, there are some that welcome the strangers and give them food and encouragement, (One of the women in the church who regularly sees angels is always loving to these people. There may be a lesson there.) and there are some that don't.

One day after the fellowship time, I had lagged behind to talk to friends and when I finally made it out of the church, there was a group of five or six people in the church parking lot gathered around an older gentleman who looked like someone who might be down on his luck. (So to speak) I walked over to the group, not saying a word to my wife who happened to be there and tried to give the "homeless" man five dollars. He looked me in the eye and said *"That's not necessary. Your wife has already given me money."* That slipped past me at the time. The fact that he knew one of these women was my wife and that it indeed was the same one that had given him money.

Also, what kind of panhandler turns down money? What he told me next kind of turned the lights on for me. He told me that his name was Harold. I asked him if he had been to any of the other churches in the area? The way he answered me was almost delivered very matter of fact, in a way that said I am on assignment. He said *"I visit all the churches in this area."* In a very business- like way. Then he thanked us and left.

I believe that Harold is an angel.

Angels Watching Over Us

One evening in 2011, my daughter Angie and I were leaving the house to go work out together and My son Matt had left with friends. My wife was busy cleaning the house. (I know. I should have probably stayed home to help her.) Not too long after we had all left, Gordana was vacuuming the stairs in the front entryway.

She was lost in her work when a man walked past her in the entryway. As he passed, she saw him from behind as he walked toward the living room.

Gordana said at first, she had thought it was me. The man was dressed in clothes like the ones I had been wearing. She said that from behind he looked very similar to me, but in better shape. That may have been what tipped her off. She then realized that I had already left the house to go to the gym. Gordana followed the man to where he had walked into the living room, but of course he was not there.

For a minute, Gordana said that she was fearful so she prayed, *"Lord I thought angels are supposed to have wings."* Gordana said that the Lord immediately spoke to her. *"No, some angels appear as men."* Then she was at peace.

This was an amazing event in our household. I believe it was either the first, or one of the very first encounters that Gordana had ever had with an angel. It increased our faith to believe for more!

The Men From El Salvador

The great thing about angels helping you is that they are always prepared. You will never hear them tell you *"Sorry, we'd love to help you but we didn't bring the right tool for the job."* Angels also don't charge you for their help. They are working for your Father on your behalf.

It was mid January and it was cold. The streets were covered in a deep snow that the snow plows had not gotten cleared away yet. The streets were slushy and messy, and ruts had been carved into the streets by the vehicles traveling over them. I was dispatched to an old industrial type neighborhood to a company to do some repairs. After I left and drove a few blocks away, I realized the my left rear tire was flat. Well, I have changed tires in bad weather before.

But I soon discovered that the truck I had been given to drive had no jack. A spare tire, but no jack. Great! To be honest I was aggravated but not completely thrown by it. I didn't know immediately what to do so I just stood there.

There was no one out and about. It was too cold. All the houses in the area were run down and appeared very uninviting to me. I was hesitant to knock on any doors.

Some movement caught my eye and I looked up. I saw two Hispanic looking men walking down an alley towards me. When they got to me, I explained I had a tire but no jack. They didn't seem very talkative at all. I thought that perhaps they didn't speak English that well, so I switched to Spanish. They were still not interested in speaking to me. One of the men told me "*wait.*" Then they disappeared back down the alley.

Not two minutes later I see them coming toward me again, but this time they are pulling a big floor jack with them. They pretty much ignored me as they changed the tire and would not allow me to help them. They didn't want me to get my hands wet and cold. After they were finished I took out a twenty dollar bill but they appeared uninterested in it and would not accept it.

Just before they left me, I asked them where they were from. They both told me twice "We are from El Salvador." Then they walked away back down the alley.

It was only later as I replayed the day's events in my mind that I realized what had happened. Two men just happened to show up exactly when I needed help. They just happened to have exactly what was needed to help me and then even though I was a stranger to them, they were still concerned about my being cold and wouldn't allow me to help. And to top it off, would not accept money.

And where, of all the places in the world had they come from? El Salvador.....The Savior. They had said "We are from the Savior."

7

ANGELS IN THE SPIRIT REALM

Sometimes you see angels in the natural realm with your natural eyes. Sometimes it will appear as if you are seeing them with your natural eyes, but in reality, you are seeing them with your spiritual eyes. And sometimes you will actually be "in the spirit" and seeing angels with your spiritual eyes.

I want everyone reading this to understand that if you desire to engage with the angelic realm, it will come to pass. All throughout the Bible believers interacted with angels. That is our standard. If you have ever been told that angels are not for today, it is only the opinion of someone who had never experienced angels and has adjusted their theology to accommodate their experience. (or lack of it.)

In the last chapter I talked about encountering angels in the natural realm. In this chapter, I will describe some events that happened in others realms and in other ways.

I mentioned early on that I would be honest about my experiences even if it doesn't show me in a good light. It's important to know that God loves us and watches over us and protects us even with all our faults.

This story, I first presented in the book "How To See In The Spirit." I believe it bears repeating.

Your Flight Has Been Cancelled

In the early days of my hunger for spiritual things, I learned that through focus and desire you can enter into the spirit realm. I also learned that in the spirit realm, almost anything is possible. We are not constrained by physical limitations. I soon learned that it is possible to fly in the spirit realm. And did I ever love to fly. I soon found myself going into the realm of the spirit only for the purpose of flying. I didn't go in for worship or prayer or fellowship with the Lord, I only went in to fly.

Angelic Encounter

On this particular day, I laid down on my bed and purposed in my heart to go into the spirit. I focused on moving into the spirit realm and after a short time, perhaps thirty minutes or so, I "shifted" into that realm. I was excited! I was in the spirit and sitting on the edge of my bed, thrilled to death and about to take flight!

All of the sudden, an angel blasted into the room. He was covered in a warrior's armor and I could literally feel an intense power coming off of him. I was in shock! His gaze was quite fierce and he actually looked like he was angry with me. He locked my eyes onto his and then told me in a very authoritative voice…

"Quit seeking the supernatural to amuse yourself! You'll open a door to the spirit of witchcraft!"

Then, as powerfully as he came, he left. It was as if a tornado had struck. The entire encounter with this angel was mere seconds, but because of the raw power of God on him and the speed of the encounter, I felt like I had just been hit by a speeding train.

The Lord corrected me and I repented.

Seek the Lord first and let all of your experiences flow out of your relationship with him.

One thing I've found about being in the realm of the spirit is that you always wish that you had more presence of mind while you are in that realm. I found this out as I sought to obey the Lord's word about going into the spirit realm to fly. Many times after this encounter with the angel, I would find myself in the spirit and still think about flying. Sometimes I would remember God's instruction and stop myself.

I'll Take You

It wasn't too long after the previous experience that I again found myself in the spirit realm and had forgotten what I had been told about flying. Right away I got all excited and said "Wow! Now I get to fly!" I was just about to take off when I remembered not to do it. I had only just said "Oh, I'm not supposed to do this", when suddenly an angel appeared on my right and said "Come on, I'll take you."

He grabbed me around the waist and took off and soon we were soaring in the heavenlies! This particular angel was quite tall, maybe eight or nine feet tall and he had light brown wings, kind of speckled with white and darker brown throughout. I didn't talk to him or ask him any questions. To be honest, sometimes I get so overwhelmed that I don't have the presence of mind to interact or ask questions. This was one of those times.

We flew over countryside and cities. We flew over many small cities and towns and over the land between them. Toward the end of our flight, the angel took me over what looked like some kind of war zone. Bombed out buildings and structures everywhere. Streets that had been torn up and destroyed. The entire city we flew over was completely desolate. I still didn't think to ask where we were or what this place was. I wish I had now.

Angelic passageway

It was a Thursday night and I prayed for a very short time before going to bed. Then I woke up at 2:30 am to fix coffee for Gordana before she went to work. (She had to start at 4 am for black Friday sale hours) After Gordana left for work, I stayed downstairs in my prayer chair and prayed until 4:30 am. Then I got up and went to bed because I didn't have to get up for work until 5:30 am.

I laid down in bed and was calling on the Lord as I was falling asleep. Suddenly I began to realize that I was in the spirit realm. In the past if I thought I might be in the spirit, I would fly. If I wasn't able to fly, then I would know that I was just awake in the natural realm. (world)

I somehow was moved into a dark and dry corridor of some sort, where all of the connecting corridors were also dark and dusty. They were not the types of places I like to be when I am in the spirit. At times I have "explored" these corridors and dark places, but I do not like such places. The only things I meet in those types of places are unclean spirits and demonic beings. As I pondered what to do, I remembered something I had heard about moving in the spirit realm. First of all, we only do those things we see the Father do. Just like Jesus did, we do the same. Also, be led of the Holy Spirit. We are not just flying around for the sake of our own amusement. We are about our Father's business. I was seeking the Lord in moving in the spirit so as I ascended, I was confident in His power to direct and protect me.

As I flew higher and higher, I flew past stars and clusters of stars. Then I found myself even above the stars and still flying higher. As I flew, I looked toward where I was flying and saw many, many spiritual beings up in the distance. As I approached them I thought that they might be demonic beings trying to stop me or attack me. I was fearful for a few seconds.

The closer I got, I realized that these beings were indeed angels and they had arranged themselves in rings of sorts, kind of like portals to travel through. There were several rings of angels that I went through, and as I got close to the top ring of angels I actually began to move right into the path of one of the angels in the ring. Once again I felt a bit of fear from this. As I braced myself for impact, I extended my arms and spread out my open palms toward him to soften the blow. But when I reached the angel, he slapped my open palms with his, kind of like giving me a high five! When he did this it propelled me even higher into the Heavens!

The Lord sets His angels around us to help us and watch over us! They are always around, always on the job.

For He shall give His angels charge over thee, to keep thee in all thy ways. (Psalm 91:11)

No Respecter of Persons

A few years ago I heard a great testimony from Prophet Bobby Conner. During a time of traveling to various places to minister, Bobby had gotten back to his hotel room a little weary and his feet were a little tired and sore.

When Bobby laid down in bed he says he began thinking about how nice it would be to have a foot massage. So he said, *"It sure would be nice to have someone rub my feet right now."* He says that all of the sudden the covers flew up to expose his bare feet and someone grabbed his feet and began rubbing! Bobby says *"I screamed like a little girl!"*

Then, Bobby yelled *"What are you doing!"* to the angel. The angel yelled back *"I'm ministering to you!"*

On the heels of Bobby Conner's testimony, I began asking the Lord for an angel to rub my feet. I know now that that request was inappropriate on many levels. But at the time it didn't really occur to me. I continued asking the Lord for the angelic foot massage for *two years!* I am glad our God is so merciful!

One night about midnight I went to my prayer chair to pray. As I sat down and settled in to pray, the thought came to me again about asking the Lord to send an angel to rub my feet. Immediately an image popped into my head. It was an image that gave me revelation and corrected my thinking.

As I sat there in my chair, an image of the Lord having spikes driven through His feet came into my mind and I was cut to the heart. I came to my senses. I told the Lord how sorry I was and that I should be the one ministering to His feet. And then I began thinking about rubbing the Lord's pierced feet. As I imagined massaging the Lord's feet, I felt revelation come upon me and I then felt an urge to look up. When I looked up I saw an angel of the Lord kneeling by my feet, and holding my left foot in his hands. He was not rubbing my foot, he was just holding it. I only saw him for a few seconds but after he was gone, I realized that my left foot was completely healed. I'd had pain in that foot for several months, but never again after that day!

Praise Jesus!

Angels Check You Out

Saturday morning I got up about 3:30 am to pray. I worshipped for a while on my knees and then prayed in tongues for an hour or so. Sometime between 5 and 5:30 am, I must have fallen asleep. I then woke up in the spirit to see "someone" looking at me with his face very close to mine.

As I realized what was going on, he slowly backed up a little, continuing to watch me and he stood up fully. He looked very much like me, but he had longer hair. An angel of the Lord. I have a feeling that he somehow pulled me into the spirit.

Guard Your Eyes

Early one morning I was praying and waiting on the Lord. As I sat there in my prayer chair, My spiritual eyes opened and I could see an angel in the distance. He looked fairly young, maybe thirty or so, and was dressed in off-white clothing and his hair was blonde and shoulder length. I could tell that he was on his way somewhere. At first, I was hesitant to engage him because I didn't want to leave the spirit realm by accident. But I decided to ask him to help me.

When he asked me *"What can I do for you?"* I could not immediately hear him, but I read his lips. I answered him *"I want my eyes to see and my ears to hear."* Then his eyes suddenly took on the look of having been injured and they were bleeding. For some reason, I thought he was trying to trick me. I said *"What are you doing? I know you're an angel of the Lord."* Then his eyes became normal again and that's when he told me, *"Your eyes and ears have been damaged by all the garbage you have put into them. But the Lord Jesus can heal them."* And then he turned and walked away.

If you are someone who is pursuing spiritual sight and fellowship with angels, be careful what you expose your eyes to. If you have a past of looking at things unclean, repent and ask the Lord to cleanse and heal your eyes.

Revelation Turns The Lights On

It was a Monday about six am. I fell into a dream and found myself talking to a dear friend. (He was a dear friend in the spirit but in the natural I didn't know him)

In the dream, I was replacing a light switch. As I worked, my friend and I talked about the Lord and the Kingdom. Most of what we discussed escaped me but I clearly remember two important things that my friend told me. He said, *"Angels can take on a different form for a season. Like a human form."* Also, I had asked him, *"What is the single greatest answer for achieving personal holiness?"* I explained to him that I wasn't talking about earning something, or achieving it by my own efforts. He said, *"The Amen."*

And then he gave me a short explanation. I believe in his explanation he was referring to Jesus as the Amen, and a relationship with Him would bring the sanctification and holiness.

My friend was a little shorter than six feet tall, trim and handsome. His hair was brown with some curl to it and not long but not short. He also spoke with what sounded like an Irish accent. I believe that even though I experienced this in a dream, the encounter was a real encounter. I believe my friend is either an angel or a member of the cloud of witnesses.

- The reason I believe the encounter to be real, even though it was dream-like is because sometimes angels have tried to talk to me and the power they carried freaked me out to the point where I could not receive the message. They have then come back later and delivered the message "couched in a dream" where I could receive it.

Walking Through Walls

One morning in January I awoke at four am. Standing by the dresser at the foot of out bed, was what I thought was "Big Bird." I know it sounds *very* strange but like anything in the spirit, if you focus, the vision does become clearer.

It was an angel. He was making me aware that my son had just gotten home. My son came into the house, walked upstairs and went into his room. (his room adjoins ours) As soon as he was in the room, the angel turned and walked through the wall into my sons room.

Angels watch over our children. Better than we do.

The Voice of an Angel

Many times the Lord has to make us aware that we don't know it all. I had seen so far at this point in my life probably several hundred angels. I had not gotten blasé about seeing angels at all. I *love* angels. But perhaps I was not giving them the respect that they are due. They are after all, beloved and powerful servants of the Lord.

As I sat in my prayer chair one morning waiting on God, I became aware of a powerful angel that was in front of me just to my left. I was not aware just how powerful until he began to speak.

As this angel spoke, the sound of his voice carried so much power that I could not handle it. The sound vibrated through me as the words hit me. The sound of his voice shook me to the core and all I could receive was... *"My name is ..... and the message is..."* I practically ran from my chair. From listening to others who encounter angels and other heavenly beings, sometimes the visitations are hard to handle. I heard Neville Johnson of The Academy of Light speak about the power of sound. He said that the rank or authority or power of an angel can be carried by their voice. Wow! I guess so!

Round Two

On the second of May, I was again in my prayer chair seeking the Lord when I fell into a dream. In my dream, I was sitting in my prayer chair praying and waiting on God.

As I waited on the Lord, I began to hear a radio broadcast that was talking about a message for the children of God, the servants of the Lord. I was actually at times a little aggravated that someone was interrupting my prayer time by playing this broadcast. I was not able to receive all of the message, but at the end of the "broadcast" I realized that I had heard that voice before. It was the voice of the angel I had been freaked out by, except this time his voice was carried to me in a dream and I could handle it!

I have since asked the Lord many times that he return and give me the opportunity to be exposed to his powerful voice again, but as yet, it has not happened. God's timing.

Angelic Explosion

A Friday in March of 2012, the Lord had me declaring in prayer according to Job 22:28. (later in the morning, Gordana told me by the Holy Spirit that I should read Job chapter 22) As Friday turned into Saturday, I was in prayer and decreeing things. I stayed in our bedroom to pray and as I did, I could hear faint rumblings in the distance of a storm that was about forty miles away from us.

Any time I hear thunder or see lightning, I always ask the Lord if He would spare one of the warriors involved in the conflict to divert towards our house and give us a breakthrough in some way. This day was no exception. Even though I could barely hear the storm, I asked the Lord for an angel of breakthrough to come.

I can't really pinpoint the time because I did not look at the clock but sometime between the hours of two and five am, I heard a faint whistling sound coming towards us from a distance. Kind of like a bomb sounds as it travels through the air. Over the course of about five seconds the sound became louder. Then a huge **Boom**! It was right over our house! When this happened, an overpowering presence entered our bedroom. I know the Lord did something significant!

Guardian Angels

Angels can be very serious and they take their jobs seriously. One morning I woke up real early and just kind of laid there in bed and asked the Lord to please show me or teach me something. I laid very still and let my eyes slowly move about the room. When I looked toward the north west corner of our bedroom, I saw a warrior standing in the corner. I only saw his back and he was just standing there facing west. When I realized what I was seeing so clearly with my open eyes I was overwhelmed. I said "Wow!" As soon as I said "Wow!" he turned and looked at me with the most serious of expressions on his face. Then he faded from view. I believe that he didn't go anywhere, he just made it so I couldn't see him. Then after a while I went back to sleep.

Angels Are Always Around

One thing that I have learned about angels is that they are encompassed around our lives. We can pray and ask God to send angels, that's true. But we always have angels as close as the thought of the name of Jesus. They are ever ready to help us and protect us.

The angel that I am aware of the most, is one who manifests his presence in some way several times a day around me. Most of the time when I am praying or talking to the Lord, he will manifest a light on my left side by my head. Just a brief flash of light, kind of an "I'm here for you" type of gesture.

Kevin Basconi, author of the "Dancing With Angels" series of books (which are amazing books that you should read) says this...

"I want to stress to you, that you do not need to be a spiritual giant or a member of five- fold ministry to see or experience the realm of angels."

But I *Really* Don't Deserve It!

Here I go again. I am about to "throw myself under the bus" but I don't mind so much because it gives me the opportunity to tell how wonderful and merciful God is. You all know I'm not perfect anyway so I might as well tell you this story.

I must start out by telling you that I don't have a problem with wine. I mean I don't have a problem with Christians who like to have a glass of wine or beer. I know it sits kind of funny with some of you, but I believe it is more of a cultural thing than anything else. I have a friend whose wife is from Germany, and some of the Pentecostal Christians there have a hard time over people imbibing in caffeinated beverages like coffee or Pepsi, but wine and beer are ok to them. Having said all that, I still don't like to have alcohol around my house. Like I said, not because I have a problem with people drinking it, but rather because of the possibility of people drinking too much and becoming drunk. That is what I don't like.

Several years ago, my son was going to have a group of friends over and they wanted to have a beer or two with their meal. He asked if it would be ok, and I said that since they were all of age I would allow it. However my fear soon became realized because three of the young people there had brought other beverages that they had hidden and by mid evening were drunk as skunks.
That *really* bothered me. I mean I was heart sick for those young people. I hurt for them that they felt like they had to be drunk to enjoy their lives. And I knew that I was responsible. Had I not allowed it, it would not have happened. I was immediately and sincerely remorseful and repentant. I told the Lord that I was sorry for not being a better testimony and for allowing it to happen. I told Him that I would not blame Him one bit if He withheld His divine protection because of this. I know drunk people get hurt sometimes and I felt that if it did happen, I probably deserved it. I was in a bad state.

Later that night, I was still talking to the Lord about it. The young people had left and I was still on this thing about "God I wouldn't blame you if you pulled back your presence from our home because of this." I guess the Lord had enough of it (my rant) because this is what happened next.

I went up to bed and was in the process of laying down to go to sleep. I laid down and was immediately caught into the spirit. The Lord then took me down to the patio area where we have the patio tables set up, where the kids had been. I was taken to one of the tables and there, seated at the table were four angels. They were all young and looked to be in their mid twenties. They were all dressed in similar clothing and all had shoulder length hair. When they knew that I had seen them, they all got up from the table and looked at me pleasantly and began to walk away. I then realized that God does not protect us because we deserve it and He does not withhold protection when we don't deserve it. He protects us because He loves us. He is a loving Father. Just as we would protect our own children whether or not they deserve it, how much more he protects us!

As these four angels began to walk away and this revelation swept over me, I asked the angels "Can I at least know your names?" Then they all turned toward me and one by one introduced themselves and shook my hand. It was awesome! Thank You Lord for mercy!

All of the angel's names were kind of strange and all of their names started with the letter m. They didn't chide or berate me. They didn't look down on me. They just smiled and shook my hand. God is good.

God is much more merciful than we give Him credit for. It is His *goodness* that leads us to repentance.

Follow The Angels

I awoke at 3:43 am and went downstairs to worship and pray. I worshipped on my knees with my hands lifted for about ten minutes and altogether for about twenty minutes. Then I sat down in my prayer chair to pray and wait on the Lord.

As I waited, I became very aware of my spirit and also the presence of the Lord. In my mind I pictured myself kneeling again with my hands lifted to the Lord. My spirit began to move and suddenly I found myself outside of our house hovering above the treetops. I tried to ascend higher into the heavens but no matter how much I willed it, it would not happen.

I stopped willing to go and just began to desire to go as high as the Lord would allow me to go. I immediately shot up into the stratosphere and was surrounded by clouds. I just began to enjoy the experience. As I looked around, I saw a group of beings in the distance traveling and carrying a bright light. At first I thought that they might be demonic but soon realized that I was seeing angels escorting souls into Heaven.

I felt drawn to them and wanted to go with them. So I followed them to their heavenly destination and wound up in a waiting or welcome area of sorts. I interacted for a very short time with one of the men in the waiting area, who told me his name and some things about his life. It was an amazing experience.

When the opportunity presents itself, follow the angels.

Angels Know How To Pray

I would like to encourage you to ask the father to send angels to minister to you. Please don't be afraid of getting out of balance. The Lord *knows* your heart and desire for Him.

He will lead you and keep you from deception. The point is that angels do know how to pray. They are very effective ministers and just as you shouldn't hesitate letting a godly person pray over you, don't hesitate accepting angelic ministry either.

One night I woke up thinking about the angelic servants of the Lord and I asked the Lord to send an angel to minister to me. I had no idea what that might look like but I knew I wanted it. As I continued looking around (actually, I was only looking around half of the room because I was laying on my side) I saw an angel approaching me. He was dressed like you would expect a knight to look and approached the bed were I lay. The last thing I remember about this encounter was him kneeling on one knee at the bedside and stretching out his hand over me. At that point I was knocked out. I don't know exactly what happened after that, but knowing the Lord, I know it must have been good!

"...You have not because you ask not." (James 4:1)

Seek And You Will Find

Many times when we wake up at night we just re-adjust our pillows and get comfortable so we can fall back asleep. I would encourage you to consider something different. If you are agreeable to encountering the things of the spirit, when you awake at night lay very still and just look around you. You never know what you might see.

One night I woke up to see a canopy of lights of sorts hanging over our bed. Upon examining the light I realized that I was looking at an angel who was hovering over our bed motionless. It was very strange and very cool. I don't think it is an accident that when your spiritual eyes open you see heavenly beings. They are always around us.

Just How Important Is Worship?

Towards the beginning of my journey into the things of the Kingdom, I sincerely tried to engage the things of God but with little understanding of how to do it. Can anyone relate? I would go on prayer walks and pray for hours, seeking direction from the Lord and also His blessing, anointing and gifts etc.. My prayers were sincere but wrong. I was planning out everything in my mind as if I had to instruct God what to do and how to do it. To make this clear, here is an example.

"Lord please cleanse me (so I can receive your infilling) and sanctify me (so I can be set aside for your purposes) and baptize me (so I can move in your power) then Lord provide me with ministry funds and provision (so I can have the means to go where I am called to go) and then open opportunities (so I can bring salvation and pray for the sick, etc.) In Jesus' name, amen." I had it all laid out for Him.

I also prayed in the best King James English I could muster up gleaned from years of exposure to people I had heard that prayed very beautiful and poetic prayers that way. (not necessarily anointed though unfortunately)

On the surface this prayer really doesn't look all that bad. That's the stuff we are supposed to be doing right? The problem here was that I was not allowing the flow of Holy Spirit in my prayer or life. I had everything planned out already of what I wanted God to do and how He should do it. What if He wanted to anoint me first and then do something else second? That's His business and all I have to be is a willing and obedient vessel. (which I now know)

After a long time of faithfully praying like this, I began to get very weary and frustrated. What more could I do? I was making myself available to God and He was not responding! I was fed up and I spent three days telling Him so!

For three days in a row I went on my prayer walk solely to talk to the Lord about my frustrations and my apparent incompetence in prayer and seeking Him. This was my new "prayer model" during that three day period...

"Lord I do not have a clue. You know I want to be like those men whose testimonies I love so much, but I don't know what to do. I know that you are probably talking to me but I can't hear you. I've spent most of my life unaware that you even still speak and I can't hear you now. Please shake me and get my attention and tell me what to do."

I prayed this prayer over and over on my prayer walks. I also would like to interject that this prayer does not qualify as vain repetition because I meant it every time I prayed it!

Of Course You Can See!

On the night of the third day something quite spectacular happened. I had done my prayer walk that day and then came home and got ready for bed. I lay down and went to sleep normally as usual.

Have you ever had an experience where someone tries to wake you from sleep by laying their hand on you and gently shaking you? Well get that picture completely out of your mind!

As I lay sound asleep, suddenly I felt someone stick their hand *into* my chest and shake me violently thus waking me up. At this point I was absolutely terrified and remember thinking *"Jesus please let this be You!"* I was immediately then fully awake and someone grabbed me by my feet and pulled me off the foot of the bed onto my knees and onto the floor. Then he grabbed my wrists and lifted my hands into a position of worship. Then he did the entire process once again. (To make sure I got the message I'm sure.) I was terrified the entire time until the end of the second time and then complete peace and wonderment came over me.

As I knelt there at the foot of my bed I looked around and saw my body lying on the bed in front of me. I realized then that I was in the spirit and I excitedly blurted out *"I can see!"* And then the angel who was now standing just to my right said in a very matter of fact manner *"Of course you can see, your eyes are open."*

That was the end of that experience because the next thing I knew was that it was morning and I was waking up. But God had indeed answered my simple prayer request in a way that I could not deny or be confused about. If you want to be like those whom God uses to do incredible exploits, be a worshipper!

If you read about King David in the Psalms, You will see the heart of a worshipper and as we know, a man after God's own heart. Let's be just like that!

Praise the Lord, all you servants of the Lord who minister by night in the house of the Lord. Lift up your hands in the sanctuary and praise the Lord. May the Lord bless you from Zion, He who is maker of Heaven and Earth. (Psalm 134)

Meeting Sam

This is an encounter that I told a couple of pieces of in the book "How to See in the Spirit".

I had just come off of a three day fast, spent praying, worshipping and waiting on the Lord several hours a day. I don't recall anything extreme happening during the fast and I didn't record anything real significant in my journal during that period. On the night at the end of my fast, I went to sleep and was enjoying a nice peaceful sleep when all of the sudden I heard someone (A man) whispering my name. "Mike...Mike!" Knowing that there was no reason for any man other than me to be in our bedroom, I got an adrenaline rush, sprang out of bed and attacked....an angel!

I did not realize at first that it was an angel because my fear/flight response was working overtime. All I could think of was protect the family and try not to get hurt too bad. As I "fought" with the angel there came a point within only several seconds that I realized that something was wrong. I suddenly realized that my "opponent" was extremely big and obviously powerful and was not fighting me seriously.

He was fake fighting with me. It was kind of like what you might do if a four year old wanted to fight with you. You would pretend and think it's funny. This angel, I finally realized was pretending to fight me and all the while laughing at me so hard it's a wonder he didn't hurt himself! When I think back on the occasion I really have a nice laugh myself.

After I calmed down and he stopped laughing, he introduced himself to me as Sam. He told me a little bit about his ministry and also relayed the fact that he was assigned during Bible school, when my parents went to a Bible college for missionaries in Waukesha, Wisconsin when I was about ten. Sam told me that he desired to have more people assigned to him, but that is a choice that we make. We decide whether to go on in the Lord or not and thus that determines the angels who are assigned to us.

Sam is quite large, probably eight and a half feet tall and very muscular. He has dark bronze skin and short dark hair. He kind of looks like a more handsome version of the Rock, Dwayne Johnson. And as you already know he has a great sense of humor, but he also has a really nice smile and a very engaging personality.

When Sam showed up he had brought me a basket filled with bread. Being overwhelmed at the time, I forgot to ask him the significance of this gift. But I asked the Lord later and He told me it was food for my spirit and soul. It was strength and nourishment, it was the word.

A Trip Behind the Scenes

I had for a long time thought that the Lord was going to give me a Land Rover as a ministry vehicle. My reasoning was that almost every time that I would be in serious prayer while out driving around, I would see a Land Rover. I would be praying up a storm and look to my right or left and lo and behold, there beside me would be a Land Rover of some sort.

So I was very excited that an angel showed up one night to take me somewhere for the ministry vehicle! He took me to a big building that looked like an airport terminal. I came to understand that this was a logistics center. As we came up to the building I saw an extended passenger van and the angel told me that it was my vehicle. When I questioned him in my mind, he explained that the Land Rover was not practical for the work the Lord had for me and the extended van would hold many more people for our purposes. I understood and agreed completely.

Then he motioned me to go with him into the building to the top. When we got to the top, we were actually on top of the building. There was a very fast paced amount of angelic activity going on. Angels with documents and papers and angels coming and going. It was a very serious and business like environment. As we stood there by the entrance door, the angel said *"Wait here."* I watched him as he walked over to a very large desk in the center of the "room" and leaned over to the angel seated at the desk and spoke something very close to his ear.

The angel at the desk, cocked his head to one side and kind of looked at me over his shoulder. It was a very, very serious look. I remember thinking that that angel looked like a very intense Gary Busey. (The actor) Very rugged, handsome and all business. He then responded to the angel who had brought me there, and went back to his other business on the desk.

After the angel with me had spoken to the other angel, his demeanor changed quite a bit. Previously he had been more serious and business like and now he had a big smile on his face as he approached me. He was genuinely excited! I could see it on his face.

He got up close to me and told me that the angel in charge had also given me a very significant gift for my ministry, and he told me what that gift was. I was stunned. I was stunned by the gift and stunned by the fact that he said it was for my ministry. I didn't even know I had one! I wish I could share a little more about that but I don't feel released to at this time.

The Land Rover

So what was the significance of all the Land Rovers that I was seeing? The Lord explained to me one day as I was driving, about the Land Rovers. They were a confirmation of my prayer, not the other way around. In other words , the Lord was telling me the my true ministry vehicle was prayer! And the Land Rovers were a confirmation of that!

I was a little hard to convince so here is what He did. After He told me that the real vehicle was prayer, a green Land Rover pulled up beside me in traffic. I said *"Lord are You really telling me that prayer is my ministry vehicle?"* And within seconds a white Land Rover passed me. I then said *"This is very strange, but if you give me one more I'll believe it."* Within fifteen seconds I stopped at a traffic light and from my left a gold Land Rover approached.

Yes indeed, my true ministry vehicle is prayer! And I don't want to be presumptuous, but I believe yours is too!

Angels in the Office

The same angel who took me to the logistics center also took me once to an office and introduced me to two other angels.

The two angels apparently had something to do with office type work and were also going to be helping me in "my ministry". I have seen some very serious members of the angelic host but it seems like the angels most closely associated with my life and family and work, the day to day stuff, have a real affection for us and a joy in what God is doing in our lives! The two angels I met in the office were as excited as the one who took me there to meet them. You can't help but be encouraged when even the angels are excited for what God is doing with you!

I don't mean to downplay the role that the serious angels play in our lives for even a moment. These guys are serious for a reason and trust me, you want them that way. When they show up radical stuff happens!

One thing that I pray for is more clarity however, more presence of mind when I am engaging with the angels. Sometimes I get so wrapped up in what they are doing or their appearance, I forget to even ask their names!

Do I Press In Or Lay Back?

I had seemingly hit a very dry patch in my relationship with God. That's the thing about experiencing the spiritual things of the Kingdom, once you have done so you want to *live* in that reality and nothing else will satisfy you.

I had been praying and reading and reading and praying, speaking in tongues, worshipping and basically throwing myself at God's feet, trying to get so very close to him. I was really at an impasse. I was seeking wisdom on what to do next to break through or whatever I was supposed to do next and I talked to someone in a position of spiritual authority . (Of sorts)

The person I talked to told me that I was burning myself out and I should take a break from all my over the top times of prayer. That God doesn't expect us to pray like that.

It's true that I was feeling kind of burned out and my flesh was in complete agreement with that word but I still sought further confirmation. Have you ever held your Bible in front of you, closed your eyes and just opened it and stuck your finger on the page? Yes, I don't recommend that either. But I confess I did something very similar. One day I was again praying concerning this and I was reading "Open My Eyes Lord" by Gary Oates. I held Gary's book in front of me and yes, I did it. I closed my eyes, opened the book and stuck my finger on the page. Here is what my finger landed on exactly.

Page one hundred and twelve has a subtitle called **"Jacob and the Angel".** In this section Gary talks about how Jacob refused to let go, and that in essence he was saying that he would not stop anything short of the full blessing of God. That is what my finger landed on when I asked if I should press in or lay back.

So now I had a dilemma of which advice to choose. Unfortunately I chose the wrong advice and fell back from seeking God in prayer. It obviously did not lead me to where I wanted to go, it only extended my dry period until God in His mercy visited me one night to make His will very plain to me on this topic.

A Prophet in Blue and Purple Robes

In this season of pondering how best to pursue God and the supernatural life in Him I desired, the Lord visited me in this way.

On a Saturday in September sometime during the night, I awoke in the spirit realm. I found myself in a very spacious room or area of some sort and the atmosphere around me was alive. I just kind of looked around in amazement like you (I) normally do in these situations. At this point the atmosphere around me was mist-like and surrounding someone in front of me. As my eyes adjusted, I saw a very tall man who at the time I perceived to be a Prophet.

This man looked like John Paul Jackson, but with longer hair and a longer beard. He was wearing beautiful, muted but glowing, purple and blue robes and there was a power emanating from him that was immense and undeniable. I then looked at his eyes and saw that they also were glowing a beautiful pale blue color. Because his eyes were glowing, I somehow thought that he must be blind. So I said to myself *"Oh, he's blind"*. Immediately an angel standing on my right side that I had not been aware of up until that point said *"No, he sees everything"*.

I was then told in my spirit that if I got into his presence, I would be blessed. And I *really* wanted that! I was ready for that dry season to be over and done!

As this "Prophet" stood there before me looking at me with those beautiful glowing eyes, I took a step toward him to stand very close to him. But when I did this, he stepped back away from me at the same time! So I again stepped forward to be close to him and he once again stepped back from me. I was a little perturbed by this but suddenly a resolve came upon me. A resolve that I *would* get close to him no matter what!

This time I did not step toward him, I lunged toward him! And this time he did not even try to step away. But because he did not step back, my momentum carried me into him and he stood there and purposely allowed me to enter into his being, or his essence! I immediately was back in my room in the natural realm with a knowledge of what I should be doing.

This was indeed a supernatural confirmation of the word given in Gary Oates's book "Open My Eyes Lord" about Jacob *not* letting go without the blessing. Take Gary's advice on this if you are also pursuing the Lord. Do not let go until you receive all that the Lord has for you!

Some Understanding

After this wonderful experience I had a clear direction but still had questions about the encounter itself. Who was this "Prophet" and what exactly did he do for starters? I decided to ask someone more experienced in these matters than I and I contacted Lyn Packer, who directs XP Media New Zealand, with her husband Rob.

She was kind and gracious enough to prayerfully lay it all out for me. I had indeed received what I thought I had, but the Prophet in the blue and purple robes (Blue Heaven, purple royalty) was none other than the Lord Jesus himself! And she explained to me why this was not a symbolic thing but a real thing. The Lord was allowing me to experience the reality of something that I knew as theology, that I am in Christ. It reminds me of what Jesus said concerning us.

At that day ye shall know that I am in my Father, and ye in me, and I in you. (John 14:20)

My Friend's Angel

Last year a friend came up to visit and I went to his hotel to hang out with him for a while. He began our visit like he usually does, by telling me what God had done recently around him. I listened to him tell a wonderful story of going to the hospital earlier in the day and ministering to various people in the waiting room and the nurses. He told me of words of knowledge that the Lord had given him concerning some of the people there. In particular, there was a nurse who my friend approached and he told her where she was from and how many kids she had and who was younger and older and also that she had been considering divorce lately and some other personal things.

Because of these words, the Lord was able to minister to this woman who received it and welcomed it.

Then, other people who had earlier rejected him as some kind of religious nut, found out about what he told the nurse and eventually all came to him asking if God could give him a word for them as well! Now that's a cool testimony!

Getting to the angel part. Within seconds of my friend standing up in his hotel room and telling me this account, a golden, glowing figure appeared behind him and made similar movements as he was moving about and excitedly telling these accounts! I have seen this particular angel twice now and both times he appeared as my friend was giving testimony.

8

DREAMS AND VISIONS

Dreams and visions are a significant part of what God is doing on the Earth today. If we are willing and aware, God can speak to us in our dreams and give us light for our path as well as destiny words for those around us.

And afterward, I will pour out my spirit on all people. Your sons and daughters will prophesy, your old men will dream dreams, your young men will see visions. Even on my servants, both men and women, I will pour out my spirit in those days. (Joel 2:28-29)

If we position ourselves before the Lord to receive, we can enjoy this blessing as well. As you read these encounters, ask the Lord to increase this in your life as well!

The Dreams Around Our Lives

For the most part when we dream, we dream about things concerning our own lives or the lives of those around us. For those who minister a lot, that has a much broader context.

The dreams I have experienced for the most part have spoken to me about personal things. For this chapter I tried to choose dreams that had a broader message that you could benefit from as well. The same applies to visions that I have had.

Warning Dreams!

The year before last, my wife Gordana and I were talking about fellowship and who we could and could not fellowship with in our lives. Was it only those people who not only love the Lord but have a desire to walk in the light or is it others as well. Certain "incidents" around our lives prompted this discussion between us. Before going to bed that night we prayed and asked the Lord to give us an answer in His word. The Lord spoke to Gordana and told her that we should read Psalm 101.

I will sing of your love and justice; to You, Lord, I will sing praise. I will be careful to lead a blameless life, when will you come to me?
I will conduct the affairs of my house with a blameless heart. I will not look with approval on anything that is vile.
I hate what faithless people do; I will have no part in it. The perverse of heart shall be far from me; I will have nothing to do with what is evil.
Whoever slanders their neighbor in secret, I will put to silence. Whoever has haughty eyes and a proud heart, I will not tolerate.
My eyes will be with the faithful on the land, that they may dwell with me; the one whose walk is blameless will minister to me.
No one who practices deceit will dwell in my house; no one who speaks falsely will stand in my presence.
Every morning I will put to silence all the wicked in the land; I will cut off every evildoer from the city of the Lord. (Psalm 101:1-8)

This was the clear word that the Lord had given us.

A Picture is Worth a Thousand Words

Sometimes we don't get it or possibly we just don't *obey* it, so the Lord has to reinforce His point. This was the dream that He gave me....

In my dream a very nice man really wanted to be my friend. He brought me to his large, beautiful home at the top of a hill and as we stood there in his large spacious living room, he offered me food and something to drink. In the dream, I could really feel that he genuinely liked me. There was no outward sign of any kind that anything was wrong.

Suddenly, ten or twelve angels appeared and surrounded me. They all began shouting *"Run! Run! Run!"* as if I was in extreme danger and could not see it. So I bolted out of the house and ran as fast as I could down the hill and away from the man and the house. As I ran, I looked back over my shoulder thinking that perhaps I would see some logical reason as to why I was running away from this man, but all I saw was the man who had now come out of the house, and was watching me with a confused look on his face as I ran away. *I knew* he didn't understand why.

But suddenly the Lord revealed to me in a sort of instant revelation as I ran, that there was something in the man that would defile me. That he could not help himself and the defiling spirits inside him would see to it if I had not run away. Therefore I could not fellowship with him.

I prayed over this dream later, trying to figure out who the man from the dream was. I did not recognize him at all and wanted to make sure that I knew who the Lord was talking about. I could think of several people in my life that the Lord might be talking about. There were people I had been witnessing to who kind of fit that description. The Lord cleared it up for me over the next ten days and it wasn't who I thought it would be.

Breaking The Bread of Fellowship

Over the next ten days, we had a fairly full calendar of dinners with friends arranged. Some in our home and some in theirs. In all, we had dinner with three different "Christian" couples all of different denominations. (which I will not disclose here) At some point in each one of those meals, as we sat there at the dinner table each one of these "Christian" men uttered something vile and profane as if it were nothing. One shouted an extremely vulgar word while telling a story he thought was humorous, one was bragging on the rich lifestyle of a friend and trying to tell me all the things (sins) he could get away with because of his wealth and one man put his hand alongside his mouth to stage whisper something vulgar to me so no one else could hear him. (but of course everyone did)

When I tried telling one man about his ungodly behavior, he *could not* receive it. One of the other men I rebuked more sharply and he got extremely angry with me, defending his actions as normal and explaining how I was the one who was out of line. The Lord made it clear to me through the Word, the dream, and the experience, that He was warning me about those who presented themselves as Christians.

Be not deceived, evil companions corrupt good morals. Watch diligently and sin not; for some do not know God. I speak this to your shame. (1 Corinthians 15:33-34)

Jealously guard your spiritual atmosphere

From the story above I would like to just reinforce to you that we have to violently guard our lives, homes and families from the defilement of the world. We have to be in this world, but not of this world. (1 John 2:15-17)

As believers we want to let our light shine upon people and even ungodly people like to feel that love that you give off.

Sometimes we want so badly for people to come to know the Lord that we tolerate really sinful behaviors because we just know that eventually they will see the light. We really have to use wisdom because many people do not want to change and until the Holy Ghost deals with them, they will not be changed. But we are not called to sacrifice our families on the altar of our compassion. We are guardians of our families and must give them a spiritual shelter and place of refreshing especially in our homes. A safe place, if you will.

Open Vision in Broad daylight

One weekday as I was out and about, I pulled into a gas station to fuel up. There was a lot of activity at the pumps that day so I had to back into a place to refuel. As I did, the backup beeper on my truck began to sound and it apparently caught the ear of the young man on the other side of the pump. As I backed into place and stopped, the young man came around to my side and smiled and saluted me. He was about twelve years old and very handsome. He actually looked very much like the son of one of my wife's friends. He was apparently refueling his mom's van when he heard the beeper and came over to check it out. As he went back to his side of the pumps, I remember thinking how pleasant he was for such a young man.

As I stood there, I heard running footsteps and a woman's voice saying *"Come on now, get in the van, we have to go now"*. I looked over and I could see the boy from behind and he was done refueling and was now running around the van playing. As he got to the front of the van, he turned and looked at me. The boy that I had seen earlier was now a boy who had the characteristics of Down Syndrome.

I was in a state of shock and frantic because I knew the mom was about to leave. *"What am I supposed to do Lord?"* I didn't know if the Lord let me see this so I would pray for the boy or what. The woman and the boy drove away.

Later as I pondered the event, I felt the Lord saying to me that I had seen the boy first in the spirit and then I had seen him in the natural. Also, I felt that He was saying that there was a day coming very soon that the we as his children would bring the manifestation of the spiritual into the natural. That we would be bringing his healing power to even those with Down Syndrome.

A Trip With Uncle Mile

My wife Gordana is originally from the country of The Republic of Macedonia. Several years ago we went there for an extended visit and I had the privilege of meeting my wife's family. All of them are amazing people! All were very loving and kind and accepting of me as I met most of them for the first time. The Patriarch, or the eldest of the family was my wife's uncle Mile. (Mee-lay is how it's pronounced) I felt a strong connection to him and feel he did to me as well. He was quiet and strong, gracious as a host, a godly man, and his grandchildren lovingly honored him in a way that was touching and spoke volumes about his character. Even though we had only known each other for a couple of weeks, before I left he gave me as a gift, a large number of beautiful lapel pins that he had collected from all over the world in his travels. I could tell that he valued them , so when he gave me some of the most beautiful ones, I could tell that he valued me as well. I was deeply honored by this.

A couple of years later I had a dream... a *very* realistic one.

In my dream I was with Uncle Mile and we were driving somewhere together in his little compact car. There was a closeness between us. The surroundings were beautiful mountain ranges like those in Lazaropole, Macedonia. Suddenly we pulled up to a large home, beautiful but not extravagant, and stopped. A woman came out of the house and walked to the car. She was happy to see Mile.

Uncle Mile turned to me and said *"I have to go now, I would like **you** to pray for the family now"*, then Uncle Mile got out and he and the woman walked back toward the house.

When I woke up I told my wife Gordana the dream and described the woman who had met her uncle. Gordana said that I described to a t, Uncle Mile's wife who had passed away a number of years earlier. It was later in the day that we received a phone call from Europe telling us that Uncle Mile had just passed away.

As one born from above, you can experience things from a heavenly dimension and you can know things that you should not know by natural reasoning. What seems strange to the world should be normal to the believer. We should be naturally supernatural. Or as Jamie Galloway says...

*"...This should be **first** nature to us. Not second nature but **first** nature..."*

Our Destiny Revealed

This vision is one that I alluded to briefly in the book "How To See In The Spirit". I will bring a bit more of it out in this account. One night as I was getting ready for bed, I had already done all the necessary stuff, had my pajamas on etc., and was seated on the edge of the bed to pray over the family and household before turning in. I was praying no special prayer, just a "God bless us and give us good sleep". While sitting there on the bed, suddenly I got a feeling that I should look up. I saw a demonic looking figure standing by our hallway door, about twelve feet away. He was dark, probably seven or eight feet tall, with big horns sticking out from the side of his head like a bull. He looked like a dark, wicked man with horns, just standing in the doorway and looking at me.

I had no idea how it gained access into our home but I was sure of one thing; it wasn't going to stay!

I rebuked it in every way I knew how and he never moved. I continued to rebuke him and after about twenty minutes he flew away.

Immediately after he flew away the space behind him (Where he had been.) illuminated and one of the most spectacular visions I have ever seen unfolded. A picture gallery of sorts that housed living paintings of my family was manifesting before my eyes. The paintings were all life sized and living! Not just life-like but actually alive. The colors were stunning and the paintings were all framed in ornate golden frames. As I entered this portrait gallery, the first painting I saw was of me! I looked at myself in this painting and I was blown away! In the painting I was wearing armor like a knight, and I had a beautiful sword and all the weaponry you would expect a knight to have. I had a very focused and intense look on my face as if I was ready or on guard for something and I was seated on a very majestic looking horse who was also covered in armor. I was in awe and speechless.

If I was speechless at seeing myself, I completely lost my breath when I moved to the next painting. All the destinies of my family were captured in that gallery and I completely understand it now when I hear people with prophetic gifts say that there is an exponential anointing on the youth of this generation. I saw it on my own children and it affects how I think about my children to this day! I could literally see and feel a very powerful anointing on the living paintings of my children. It was awesome! It was literally *ten times* what I had seen in my own painting!

Blocking the Vision

That demonic thing had been blocking the vision that the Lord wanted me to see. That's one of the things the devil does, he blocks your vision if he can. God also has a destiny for you and your children. It is so awesome and profound that when he shows it to you, you may still have a hard time comprehending it.

Ask the Lord to show you how He sees your children and it will change the way you see them and think about them forever!

It's All a Dream

Very often those of us who pursue the supernatural things of God have an adjustment period when it begins to manifest in our lives. Because we don't start out with any experiential knowledge of things like angelic visitations or trans-relocation or being in the spirit, we relegate such things to "dream" status. No matter what we really experience, we believe at first that it is some sort of dream rather than some sort of spiritual reality. Things will become more apparent of what they truly are the more we experience them.

As we experience things more and more, we become more aware and can engage the deep things of God more fully. I would also like to suggest that if you are taking this journey (and I hope you are) invest in a journal and record every supernatural thing that happens in your life. If you do so, you will gain understanding more quickly and also the fact that you are honoring the things that God is doing will cause them to increase in your life as well.

Bruce Allen has many resources that talk about moving in the spirit realm such as the book Translation by Faith and Foundations of Glory.

Gordana's Troubling Dream

One Saturday morning upon waking my wife Gordana told me about a very disturbing dream that she had just dreamt. She had seen the walls of our home were all made of concrete and they were covered with vile and ungodly pictures and artwork. She was a little more graphic than I will be here.
Later in the morning I was in prayer, and felt that I should ask the Lord about what Gordana had seen. After a short

time I felt that I was hearing the Lord respond to me about the dream. He didn't really explain anything to me, but rather gave me a very strange instruction to carry out. Here it is...

"Take a hammer and strike the floor, and when you do, the three angels with you will strike the floor at the same time and the concrete walls will be broken and the evil will be routed out and there will then be nowhere for them to hide".

I don't mind telling you that I sincerely questioned if this was God or if it was some crazy thing that my own mind had come up with. I thought about hitting the floor with a hammer and I knew if I did that the floor tiles would break and I didn't think I would be able to convince my wife that God told me to break our floor tiles! Thankfully the Lord explained to me that this was to be a "prophetic gesture" and I would not use a physical hammer but a spiritual one.

I then went through the physical motions of taking a hammer from someone I couldn't see, and then I made the motion of striking the floor with the invisible hammer. It seemed very strange to me at the time because I had very little knowledge of or experience with prophetic gestures. But I did it anyway.

Later in the day I sat down to read the Bible. When I laid the Bible down on our kitchen table, I randomly flipped it open towards the middle because I had intended to read a Psalm.
However I looked at the page heading of where I had randomly opened the Bible and it said "Prophecy". I thought to myself *"I love prophecy so I'll just read this"* The chapter I had randomly chosen was Amos chapter nine. This is a part of what it says...

(Vs.1) I saw the Lord standing upon the altar and He said, Smite the lintel of the door, that the posts may shake , and

cut them in the head, all of them, and I will slay the last of them with the sword: he that fleeth of them shall not flee away and he that escapeth of them shall not be delivered... (Vs.3) And though they hide themselves in the top of Carmel, I will search and take them out thence...

This scripture was too close to what I had just experienced to be a coincidence. And beyond that, Carmel is the name of the city where I live!

Sometimes when you have dreams about your life or home or your family, it's the Lord giving instruction on how to pray. Anytime you see things in visions or dreams that appear to have no relation to real life, ask the Lord to clarify things for you. If you see anything that has any hint of the devil's handiwork, pray against it whether you feel it is significant or not. I am not sure we ever experience anything insignificant as Christians seeking to serve the Lord. Those who are willing for God to move in supernatural ways in their lives can expect to experience things that stretch them. The more willing you are to let God be the boss, the more He will stretch you!

...Your old men shall dream dreams, and your young men shall see visions...(Joel 2:28 & Acts 2:17)

And God did extraordinary/special/unusual miracles by the hands of Paul. (Acts 19:11)

Let God do the unusual through you.

Ministry Dreams

If you pray for others God will give you dreams and visions of instruction concerning the lives of others. He will tell you how to pray for them and or what they are going through in their lives. Sometimes the Lord will show you what sins they are bound by or He will give you very specific words to deliver to those He is calling to repent.

Several times I have asked the Lord how to pray in certain situations and I see in my dreams, people doing the most ungodly things. Things I really don't want to see, but I know God has a reason for showing me. Many times I have been instructed to deliver a word I did not really want to deliver but sometimes people's souls are at stake if they are not brought to repentance. A supernatural word from God will sometimes shake people up enough that they will reconsider giving themselves to ungodliness and they will repent. We must follow the Holy Spirit and walk in love.

Dreams and Clarifications

One of the coolest things that the Lord does sometimes is to tie seemingly random things together so perfectly that it could never be a coincidence. I have seen the Lord do this many times and this next story is just a neat example of that, while also featuring one of my favorite people Prophet Bobby Conner.

One night I had a very realistic dream where my wife Gordana and I were sitting comfortably in our home, when suddenly there was an excitement of some sort happening outside. We could hear muffled shouting and suddenly there came a loud insistent knocking on our door. When I answered the door, there was a fireman standing there in all his gear and he shouted to us *"Come out here! There are fires burning everywhere!"*.

I walked outside and sure enough there were fires everywhere! There were fires burning in the streets and in the yards all about the size of a fire that you might have in your fire pit. Lots and lots of fires! The landscape was completely covered with these fires. I asked *"Who is setting all these fires?"* I looked at the fires and went back into the house and told my wife that we don't have to worry, we will be safe.

The following afternoon I had a little time so I got on Youtube and searched for a Bobby Conner video to watch. I came across one I hadn't seen so I hit play and settled in. All of the sudden on the video, Bobby Conner is shouting *"There are fires burning everywhere!"* I was pleasantly stunned! I then listened to Bobby explain that the Lord is digging holes. He is digging out all of the filth and unclean from us, like out of a pit, and filling us with the oil of the Holy Ghost and then setting us on fire! He is cleansing us and getting us ready to use us! The fires are us! God is setting us on fire!

God gave me the message twice, once in a dream and once with perfect instruction and clarification to make sure I got it. He wants us to get it so He can bless us and use us like we want to be used! He is so good!

9

MOVING IN THE SPIRIT REALM

And he gave orders to stop the chariot. Then both Phillip and the eunuch went down into the water and Phillip baptized him. When they came up out of the water, the spirit of the Lord suddenly took Phillip away, and the eunuch did not see him again, but went on his way rejoicing. (Acts 8:38-39)

If you make yourself available to the Lord, He will do for you what He has done for others and that means He will move you supernaturally for His purposes. As You can see from the scripture above, He did it for Phillip. But He also did it for Elijah. (2Kings 2:16) Obviously the prophets knew something about the Lord transporting Elijah or they would not have mentioned it in Second Kings.

More recently Padre Pio of Pietrelcina (1887-1968) has a long, documented history of moving in the spirit for ministry purposes. There are scores of witnesses that attested to the fact that he had on numerous occasions, preached or ministered at two different locations simultaneously!

Even more recently, there are reports of preachers in China who hold conferences (illegally) and when the authorities come to arrest them, they are hundreds of miles away! Also I heard a report of a Russian pastor who preaches at two different churches, who the Lord has been moving supernaturally because the churches are so far apart!

To hear testimonies from people currently being used in this way by the Lord, one need only to listen to Jamie Galloway, Patricia King, Dennis Walker, John Paul Jackson and Bruce Allen, to whom the Lord has given a mandate to teach this for end time ministry!

So as I share my personal testimonies, please know that this and far greater is available to *you!* As you read these stories I would encourage you to tell the Lord *"I am willing to do that Lord!"*. As you know, the Lord Himself has qualified you and also told you all throughout the Word that we are to desire spiritual things and set our hearts on the things above which are eternal. Don't be left out of this! As I heard missionary to Mexico David Hogan say recently, *"There's some weird stuff goin' on. You're either gonna get with it or you're gonna get washed out of the way"*. Let's all get with it!

Early Adventures

I had heard some great testimonies about servants of the Lord moving supernaturally to minister, particularly from Bruce Allen, Patricia King and John Paul Jackson. At this point so far as I knew, I had not actually experienced this or even asked for it but I do remember thinking about how cool it would be to do that! Kind of like how I used to feel as a kid when I would hear all those great Bible stories in Sunday School of God doing the most outrageous things and thinking *"wouldn't it be awesome if God still did that stuff!"* Little did I know at the time that He still did, and still does!

One night after being asleep for several hours, I woke up standing in what looked like a third world hospital of sorts.

There were ten or twelve beds in the room and all of the beds were occupied by children. I walked through the room down the line of beds to each and every bed and touched each child on the head and said *"Be healed in Jesus' name"*. To the child in the last bed, I touched his head and said *"Be healed and delivered"*. I could see other rooms filled with children also but did not go into them. After I had prayed over each child in the room, I found myself back home.

Even though the experience was realistic and I walked through it with my faculties functioning, I still at the time had thought that it was some kind of very realistic dream. (Early on I had thought *everything* was a dream) The Lord gave me greater awareness about such things as time went by.

After I began to pursue spiritual things and the Lord had allowed me to experience some things in the day when I could not deny that I was indeed awake, I began to engage this on purpose by using stillness and imagination to enter in. At first I began to sit in my prayer chair and purposely see myself leaving my chair, flying to some small hospital somewhere (Because my first experience was a hospital) and then going from room to room praying for people. I would then tell the Lord *"Lord I am willing to do this if You want me to"*. It wasn't long before this began to open up over me, perhaps two or three months.

The order in which I experienced certain things is not always known to me because when I record things in my journals, unfortunately sometimes I will notate the weekday and time, but not necessarily the date.

The second trip was much like the first one. While waiting on the Lord, I suddenly found myself moving somewhere and ended up in front of a "hospital" of sorts, somewhere in eastern Europe. The building was a pale blue color and had concrete walls in some disrepair.

There were five or six steps at the entrance and I walked up the steps into the hospital. Upon entering, I could see that there was no information desk or entrance desk of any sort and I could see no one in the halls . I went into the first room on the right and saw an older man in his bed, alone and too ill to move much. The room was almost completely bare, with only the bed, a small end table and a chair next to the bed on the left. He watched me as I walked over to him. I didn't know what language he spoke so I just spoke to him in tongues hoping that the Holy Spirit would tell him what He wanted him to know. Then I knelt beside his bed and laying my hands on him I began to pray. As I prayed over him the Lord gave me some words of knowledge about his life and the fact that his wife really needed him to live and he wanted to live so he could take care of her.

I prayed over him for quite a while and after I felt that I was done, I stood up and smiled at him, kissed him on top of the head and walked out of the room.

The Russian Elevator Repairman

This ministry trip also happened during the night watch. One night I suddenly found myself standing in the hallway of a large apartment building. Not far from where I stood there were was an elevator and middle aged man standing on a ladder working on it. I walked over to him. I began telling him that Jesus loved him and He wanted to give him good things. I told him that several times and he actually started to get very angry with me. I was also led to touch his arm as I told him the Lord loved him. He sensed that I was doing something to him and began to come down off the ladder. Because of the look on his face, for a moment I thought he might hit me. But suddenly as he came off the ladder, he broke down and became very emotional and yielded to the Lord. It was a very, very neat thing! Also, during the course of talking to the man (we were speaking in Russian) he used a word that I did not know. It was the word "razresheniye".

It has been a long time since I studied Russian and I don't use it enough to be fluent and I told him that I didn't know that word. He spoke some English and told me the word meant "understanding". After I got back, I went to the computer and discovered that it indeed meant understanding. The Lord could have easily allowed me to have an "understanding" of that word, but I believe the Lord allows little glitches like this so you will know that He is really doing this. He wants us to be aware of that fact.

I also had some understanding that the man's wife had been praying for him and the Lord was answering her prayer.

A Sad Young Man

Early one Thursday morning in April, I found myself standing in front of a little house in a nice quiet neighborhood . The weather was very pleasant and reminded me of California, although I'm not sure exactly where it was.

I went up to the door of the house and knocked, and a young Hispanic man about twenty-five years old came and opened the door and then immediately closed it. He was acknowledging that I was there and at the same time telling me that he didn't want to be bothered. I banged hard on the door and he again came to the door. I quickly told him "I'm supposed to pray for you". I relayed the fact that I knew that he was sick and dying, and that he just wanted to be left alone to play his piano and enjoy his music for whatever time he had left. He allowed me to come in and pray for him.

We were still standing not far from the door in the living area and I laid my hand on his chest and began to pray. Almost immediately a demon manifested and I began casting out demons, calling them to come out. I then placed my hand on the young man's throat and continued ministering deliverance. I began kind of softly and gradually got louder. Eventually I just found myself back home without having any awareness of the transition.

The Lord made me aware though that He had healed the young man and I was very happy that He had allowed me to be a part of it.

I would encourage every person reading this to ask the Lord to use you in this way. There are people all over the world who are lost and dying or sick, and they have no one around their lives to pray for them. Many of them are alone. God will make a way to help them because He loves them and He will use you if you are willing. Tell Him you are willing.

Checking Up On The Kids

Late one evening I began to be worried about my daughter being out with her friends. I had called her several times and she had not answered or called me back. I don't want to sound like the classic overly protective dad, but perhaps I am sometimes.

Towards bed time I decided to pray a bit more seriously about the situation. *"Lord help me to at least know she's alright"*. As I laid down to go to sleep, suddenly I found myself flying over neighborhoods and houses and I realized that I recognized the area. I came to a little town called Brownsburg and then found myself flying lower to the streets over Brownsburg. I then saw a street called Green Street and made a left and flew down that street. I then came before a house and saw the numbers on the house and entered the house, still in the spirit realm.

I walked into the living room and saw my daughter and four of her friends sitting in the living room talking and hanging out. The Lord had allowed me to see that she was ok.

The next day I told my daughter that I had been worried about her and she apologized. I told her it was ok because the Lord had allowed me to see that she was ok and then I told her the address of where she had been and I described what the living room looked like and what they had been doing.

My daughter was excited but only mildly surprised because when you live in an atmosphere of the supernatural, it becomes natural to you. But her friend that had gone with her was a bit freaked out by it!

Sometimes we are concerned over our loved ones and we don't know if they are ok or even how we should pray for them. But as sons and daughters of God we have resources that we can lay hold of by faith. I would encourage you to lay hold of this testimony's power for your own life when you are in a similar circumstance.

Equal Opportunity

Since I told the preceding story about my daughter, let me tell you one about my son.

One night my son was spending the night at a friend's house. I had never been to the house but I had met the parents and felt that it was a safe environment so I was not worried at all. After I went to sleep, I woke up standing in a basement- like entertainment room looking at my son laying sound asleep on a dark brown couch. There was a big screen TV on the other side of the room and I could see through a window, a yellow van parked on the street in front of the house.

As I stood there in the room, the Lord told me that the man in the van was up to no good and I was to pray . So I stood there in that strange house breaking the power and plans of the enemy concerning the person in the yellow van. Then I came back home.

The next day I talked to my son and told him what had happened. I described the room and told him that I had seen him sleeping on the couch there. He verified that the room was as I had described it and that he had fallen asleep on the couch and had slept there. He did not recall seeing a yellow van outside but had not really looked for one either. The Lord protects us even when we are not aware we need it.

Deliverance From Dark Places

Several years ago someone I love very much was diagnosed with a very aggressive life threatening disease. After a battle of a couple of years, he was told by the doctors that they had done all that they could and he had perhaps a couple of months to live. I was led to fast and pray. I had heard so many testimonies of God's healing power, I felt I had to petition the Lord again even though I had already prayed for his healing many times.

Originally I felt led to fast for two weeks but at day thirteen the Lord told me I could eat, so I did. Later that night my spiritual eyes opened and I was taken to a place, or region of captivity in the spirit realm. I walked down hallways in the spirit until I came to a room where I saw the soul of the one who was ill. I could see why he was ill. The Lord made me aware that there was a demon who was making this person ill and I was to command him to tell me his name. The demon told me his name and I then commanded him to go. When the demon came out of him I was very surprised by his appearance. While this evil spirit was in my friend his appearance was ugly, but when he came out his appearance was extremely beautiful. Wicked and beautiful. I could easily see why the Word says that Satan transforms himself as an angel of light. The demon immediately but unwillingly obeyed the command the Lord had me give. As he was going away, I heard a voice far away say "I feel so sorry for him (my friend) sometimes I wish it was me instead". When the evil spirit heard those words he turned and smiled an evil smile at me and was gone. I knew that he had found a new home.

A week after this experience my friend was retested by his doctors. They could find no trace of the disease. In the wake of the incredible news I found that some people surrounding his life called his healing a miracle and others believed that his medicine finally "kicked in" and did its' job. I'm believing the former rather than the later.

A Trip To See Joseph

When you wait on the Lord you can enjoy some incredible adventures! Most of the really cool stuff the Lord shows me happens when I am waiting on the Lord in stillness. This missions trip is no exception!

On this particular night I had pretty much waited, prayed and worshipped all night and morning was almost upon me. (I said this in my other book but I'll repeat it. I'm not trying to impress you by telling you that.) I normally pray through the house before I turn in but this time I had just planned on going to bed. It was past four am and I got up from my prayer chair and went in the kitchen to get a drink. I then saw that the basement light was on so I called downstairs but got no answer. I decided that before I turned in I would just step outside for a minute and get a breath of the morning air and then turn in. So I walked to the side door of the house and then stepped outside.

When I stepped outside, I was in another place. I was literally standing in front of a church somewhere where there were lots of people milling about, gathered for some kind of conference that was going on. I looked around in amazement and drank it all in. I remember thinking *"This has got to be the coolest thing yet!"*

I looked across the lawn of the church and saw a black man who appeared to be about my age with gray around his temples. I somehow knew that this man's name was Joseph. At that moment, the Lord made me aware that He had put money in my pocket and I was to give it to Joseph. I walked over to him and handed him the money and said *"This is for you"*. And then I began to walk away. He suddenly yelled after me *"Hey! This will buy three containers of food!"* He was very excited!

Next, realizing that the Lord had transported me there to do this "Kingdom Mission", I decided to try to find out where I was and who this Joseph was. I figured that I could look it up on the internet when I got home! I saw two women talking nearby so I approached them. *"What can you tell me about Joseph and his ministry?"* I asked. One of the women responded to me by saying *"Oh you'll find out all about him, he'll be here all week. But let us pray for you"*. Then these two women laid hands on me and prayed a really great prayer over me, prophesying among other things visitations from the Lord and from the Prophet Enoch!

Right after that prayer the Lord brought me back and I wound up back in my prayer chair with waves of electricity coursing through my body for twenty to thirty minutes. It was absolutely awesome!

Are you encouraged you to wait on the Lord yet? I hope so!

The Witchdoctor's Stump

Very early one morning I was waiting on the Lord when I began seeking the Lord about moving somewhere in the spirit to pray for someone perhaps. After a while I began to move in the spirit and found myself going somewhere. I thought perhaps another hospital but wound up standing in the middle of a village of small mud and straw houses (huts) in what I believe may have been Africa. The ground was barren and dry , a reddish-brown color and the village looked deserted. There was a hut directly to my right and I felt that I should enter it. When I did, I saw a man and a woman standing close to the doorway who apparently had been watching me. I looked to my left and saw a little girl who appeared to be very sick. I squatted down and extended my hand toward her and commanded sickness to leave.

After I had prayed for her I looked again at the man and the woman and exited their little home. As I came back out I noticed an old tree stump in the center of the village and I was led to go stand on it and begin preaching the gospel.

As I preached, I noticed people coming out to see what I was doing but they all stayed far away. I continued preaching and I was aware that I was preaching in English, but it wasn't coming out that way. I knew that they all understood me. After less than fifteen minutes the little girl I had prayed for came out of her hut and came and sat on the edge of the stump I was preaching from.

When the little girl sat down, the people slowly began moving forward toward us and soon they were quite close. As all the people moved forward, the couple from the hut I had been in also came and stood in the small crowd of maybe forty or fifty people. Many people gave their hearts to the Lord. I also became aware that the reason the people were afraid to come forward to where I was standing was because I had been standing on the witchdoctor's stump. No one stood there but him. I haven't been back there to that village but would like to visit again if the Lord wills.

A Region Of Captivity

One night I awoke in the spirit to find myself in a very bleak dark place. The terrain was a little bit hilly and barren and I was standing on a small hill, kind of hidden. Down in a small valley of sorts there was a huge iron gate. Behind the gate were hundreds if not thousands of women all packed in behind this gate face outward. They all had expressions on their faces that conveyed hopelessness and despair. Standing in front of, but outside of the gates, was Prophetess Ana Mendez Ferrell. She had her hands outstretched toward the gates and was apparently doing warfare on behalf of those women. I then also stretched out my hands and began to pray but I stayed where I was on the hill, hidden from view.
There is a book called "Regions of Captivity" by Ana Mendez Ferrell that is a must read for anyone who is in ministry. If you are in the deliverance ministry this resource will be especially helpful. Regions of captivity are places in the spirit realm where parts of one's soul can become imprisoned.

This can happen from a number of different ways, such as sins, traumas, curses, or even events from previous generations. Many times people cannot receive or hold their deliverance because their souls are still imprisoned.

Here is a personal example from my own life that I also told in my book "How to See in the Spirit".

Out Of The Dungeon

The first experience I had with the regions of captivity was my own personal deliverance from some type of "coldness" that was affecting my emotions toward my wife and daughter. Here is a little back story...

For some time, perhaps a year or more, I had been feeling an emotional distance between me and my wife and daughter. I could think of no logical reason for this. I loved them both dearly and wanted to show them the affection that I felt. But there was a coldness of some sort that kept me from feeling that closeness.

One night in the middle of the night I awoke to find myself in a small enclosure like a prison cell with a barred door. I was wide awake with all my faculties and this was in no way just a bad dream. The iron bars of the cell door were on fire. As freaked out as I was by all this, the Lord had still given me the presence of mind to use the name of Jesus. I raised my hand and struck at the door as if I had a sword, two times. I shouted *"fall in the name of Jesus"* twice also.

The door fell and I walked out of the cell, up a long narrow stairway out of a dark place, through a door and into the light. I immediately saw my wife and daughter and they were glowing beautifully. I was completely restored to them.

The Door Of Intercession

One evening I began to be very worried about a loved one who lived far away. I know we are not supposed to worry but pray instead, but It was the worry that drove me to prayer.

I went into the bedroom and hit my knees. I began to pray but because I didn't know exactly what I should be praying for, I prayed in tongues. I also prayed with a great intensity because of the burden I felt. After about four hours the burden began to lift and as it lifted I felt my spirit begin to move and I was transported to the home of the person I had been praying for. I was standing in the same room with the man in the midst of a party. I could see everything in the natural and the spiritual. The atmosphere was not good. There were demons openly walking through the crowd of people without fear as if they owned the place.

Thinking that the Lord brought me there to deal with them, I found the largest one and began to rebuke him. He was unfazed and never even looked at me. I continued to rebuke him and at one point I said *"Can you not hear me!"* And then he slowly turned to look at me and as if he was bored said *"Yes, I can hear you"*. And then he turned and walked away from me to another place in the room.

Later I confirmed all the things I had seen that night (in the natural realm of course) with the man I had been praying for and he told me that yes, there had been a party going on and the scene was as I had described it.

I realized that the Lord had taken me there so that I would know what was going on and how I should intercede. The Lord also taught me that I had limited authority in that place. Yes I could intercede on the man's behalf but he also has a free will. If he chooses to invite demons into his home, he has every right to do so.

Go In The Spirit & Pray In The Spirit

Waiting on the Lord is one of my favorite things to do. There is no telling what may happen when you wait on the Lord. Waiting in stillness is the key. Bringing your thought life under subjection and just letting your time and your focus be all about Jesus.

The supernatural of God then becomes very accessible.

Many times after I am done praying and waiting on the Lord at night, I will go through the house and pray over the rooms. After walking around through all the rooms and pleading the blood of Jesus or placing the house under the power and protection of the Holy Spirit, or praying in tongues, I have gone back to the original place where I started, only to discover that my body never went with me. I was actually in the spirit as I walked through my house praying in the spirit!

One night I had laid down on the floor in our bedroom to pray because it's easier to stay awake on the floor, as the surface isn't as comfortable as a bed. (obviously) I fell asleep on the floor anyway and decided that I should get up and walk around the house and pray, because it would definitely be hard to fall asleep as I'm walking. So I got up and began going room to room praying over the household. I got back to my room and you guessed it, my body was still lying there on the floor beside the bed! So I went back to my body and *eventually* made it to bed.

I say eventually because sometimes when you are in the spirit you may have a hard time bringing your physical self to wake up. At first if you have no experience in this area, you can be fearful. I was. The first time it happened to me I began thinking *"what if I never wake up!"* and I was more than a little fearful. I kept shaking myself as hard as I could until I finally woke up. When you navigate the supernatural realms you really become very aware of just how dependent you are on Jesus, and just how powerful His name really is!

When You Go In The Spirit

Many of you reading this book probably already experience many of the things that I have talked about and others of you really desire to or have just started to. There is always an adjustment period. That's why many times you read in the Bible where an angel says *"Don't be afraid"*. They say that because they know we are not used to this.

"...don't be afraid.." (Luke 2:10)

It's Not The Same

Many times when you are in the spirit, things will not appear as you believe that they should. You will walk through your house and the atmosphere will be different. There will be objects that you see that you know are not *really* in your house. Or you will see furniture missing or the colors are different etc.. You may then believe *"I must be in a dream because my house doesn't really look like this"*. And indeed sometimes it might be in a dream.

But what you are seeing is your home in the spirit realm. Sometimes you will see both realms, the natural and spiritual and sometimes just the physical. That's why the appearance is different. Once I opened my eyes in the spirit to see a bed guard rail of sorts mounted to my side of the bed. I haven't used a guard rail like that since I was little!

Many times what you see will be a reflection of the current spiritual atmosphere in your home. If things look bleak, just start worshipping more in your home and singing praise songs. It will change the environment!

10

DARK THINGS

For we wrestle not against flesh and blood, but against principalities, against powers, against the rulers of the darkness of this world, against spiritual wickedness in high places. (Ephesians 6:12)

Long before I had ever seen an angel, I had seen devils. My knowledge of the reality of the demonic had actually started though, when my parents were in Bible college preparing to become missionaries.

One evening there appeared to be something going on in the dormitories were we lived and we kids were all told to stay in our rooms. Later we found out this story. Two of the girls from the college were studying together in their room when they began talking about conviction of sin by the Holy Spirit. One of the girls said that she felt no conviction whatsoever when she sinned. Her roommate began asking her questions about it and soon the girl who felt no conviction began talking in a man's voice and then soon after that began talking in several men's voices and all of them (the men's voices) began arguing with each other. The other girl ran to get help, and then some of the elders cast the demons out of her. The demons didn't go too far. One floor up in the men's dorm they entered into one of the male students and the elders then had to repeat the process. Of course God's power won the day and both were delivered by His almighty power!

Both of those kid's had made a commitment to Christ and were in Bible College preparing to serve the Lord. This scenario really put a dent in that whole theory that says demons can't afflict Christians. I guess that's why our Lord tells us *"Neither give place to the devil". (Ephesians 4:27)*

My Own Testimony (The Short Version)

I could give a very similar account myself. After accepting the Lord as my savior at five years old, I began earnestly witnessing and trying to lead others to Christ. I began to drift away from the Lord as I got older and in my teen years and early twenties lived a sinful life, full of all the things the world calls normal. You know, "boys will be boys", and "sowing my wild oats" etc.. Which are *"cute"* ways of saying "living in sin". I was giving place to the devil.

In my early twenties I was in such bondage to the devil that I didn't know what to do except cry out to God. He answered my cry and sent a someone to my aid. A man whom I had never seen before walked up to me and told me the four things that were tormenting me, and he was very precise and correct. There was no natural way that this man could have known what I had been praying. Then he told me that God had told him to pray for me, which he did. I was also delivered by God's mighty power!

Behold, I give unto you authority to tread on serpents and scorpions, and over all the power of the enemy, and nothing shall by any means hurt you. (Luke 10:19)

Once I was *really* aware of the reality of the devil and of how he could afflict you if you gave him the opportunity, I tried to live a clean life, pleasing to the Lord. It was a process though.

Opening The Hedge Of Protection

Sometimes we do things that we know are wrong. They even *feel* wrong, but we do them anyway. This is such an occasion.

It was close to midnight and my wife Gordana had already put the kids to bed and gone to bed herself. I had stayed up to relax, drink coffee and watch TV in the garage / family room for a while. For the most part I was watching Christian TV but on occasion I would channel surf to see what else was on. I just happened to come across a popular werewolf movie that had just come out on TV, and I watched it for a few minutes. I began to feel convicted for watching though because of the sheer wickedness of the "hero" of the film, so I changed the channel. However, ten minutes later I again began to watch the show and again felt the conviction of the Holy Spirit and again changed the channel.

You would think that I would have gotten a clue, but no. A little later I once again turned back to the werewolf movie and began watching it. This time, after just a couple of minutes I heard a blood curdling scream coming from the far end of the house from my daughter's room. I ran to her room and found her terrified, cowering and crying. She kept screaming *"There's a wolf in my room! There's a wolf in my room!"*

You could literally feel the evil presence in the room. I felt very, very low at having subjected my daughter to demonic attack because of my disobedience and I repented profusely. Repentance was a starting place but it still took about two hours of prayer to drive out the evil presence and restore enough peace to my daughter so that she could sleep. I had opened the hedge of protection.

Am I saying that even watching the wrong movies can open a door to the devil? Absolutely yes, no doubt about it. We don't have to be in fear though.

If you are watching something that you shouldn't, the Holy Spirit will convict you and bring you around. If you don't feel conviction, many times God's grace will keep the hedge around you until you learn better. But if you feel the conviction and repeatedly reject it like I did, you are opening a door and making an invitation. You don't have to ask twice. So the Lord was in the process of teaching me that devils can and do bother Christians. I also learned that they have no qualms whatsoever about tormenting children.

Demons Don't Like You

As I began to learn about warfare and deliverance, I learned that demons don't like you even when you are not confronting them. If you are walking in the Spirit, the Holy Spirit within you makes the atmosphere unbearable for them and they react.

One day my wife and I were in a doctor's waiting room, sitting quietly awaiting our turn. Suddenly a little boy about five years old came and stood in front of Gordana and began growling, *"I hate you!"* And as he would say this he would kick at her. Equally as strange, his mother who was sitting nearby never said a word.

I know many don't believe that the devil can bother kids because it's so unfair. Yes it is unfair and that's why we have to make our families and our children off-limits by using the authority that God has given us. (Luke 10:19)

IF YOU FORGET EVERYTHING YOU LEARNED THIS WEEKEND, JUST REMEMBER 'COME OUT IN JESUS' NAME' AND YOU'LL BE OK.

Hegewisch Baptist Church – Deliverance Conference 2010

Alien Entities

Dr. Lester Sumrall used to have a program on TV called "Alien Entities" that I would watch and study along in the study guide. I learned a lot and also realized that "alien" is a good, descriptive word for devils. It fits.

At this time in my life I was spending a good deal of time in Bible study and prayer. Up until this point I had never actually seen a demon or evil spirit to my knowledge. I had heard them speak through people and some times that can be kind of freaky.

On this particular day I was in my bedroom praying, although I don't recall what about, when I suddenly felt drawn to look up. When I did I saw a demonic snake-looking creature about the size of a man standing in the doorway of the bedroom. He had a very angry look on his face and just stood there looking at me and I in turn just looked back at him. I didn't have any fear in this however. I was a bit stunned but not fearful. I was just watching him when he suddenly rushed at me. I experienced the whole thing almost as if it were a slow motion sequence in a movie. I can still see it as it's kind of hard to forget!

As this thing rushed at me, he got to within a couple of feet of me when it looked as if some invisible force knocked him for a loop! A look of shock replace his angry look and he retreated quickly. Yay God's angels!

I was kind of surprised that I was not afraid during this encounter, but what I have found is that God gives us grace in these circumstances to deal with things that we would not be able to handle apart from Him.

...For this purpose the Son of God was manifested, that He might destroy the works of the devil. (1 John 3:8)

Freedom

There is nothing like it when God uses you to set someone free. No earthly accomplishment can compare to it. The times when everything falls perfectly into place, orchestrated by the hand of God and you get to be a part of it.

My wife and I were visiting another church in our city on this particular Sunday. As we sat in our pew, somewhere up toward the front there was a commotion taking place. We then watched as several deacons went up and helped a young boy out of the sanctuary to the back of the church. At the time we thought that perhaps the boy had fainted or fallen. I found out about an hour later that the boy had been having seizures due to what he claimed was an evil spirit. His parents had taken him to the best medical specialists in our city and they had not been able to help him.

Of course from a medical perspective, the seizures were causing the hallucinations or the hallucinations were causing the seizures, but either way the whole premise of an evil spirit at work was not considered. The situation had gotten so bad that the doctors had said that his life was in jeopardy due to the increasing severity of the seizures. I knew that the boy was telling the truth and I wasn't sure how the parents would react, but I had to offer to pray for him. I knew that feeling of torment and hopelessness only too well.

His parents said yes, I could come over and pray. The drive there took me about an hour and I prayed in tongues the whole way. I was angry and I set my resolve that God would indeed give this boy deliverance this day! When I arrived the family met me at the door and invited me in. I wasn't real sociable because I was focused on the task at hand. I immediately went over to the dining room, grabbed a chair and put it in the middle of the living room and told the boy to sit in it. I explained to him that the angels around him were far greater in power than any evil spirit and that the authority of Jesus' name would set him free.

After I had talked to the boy for a minute assuring him that it would all be ok, I addressed the evil spirit and commanded it to leave. Immediately the boy expelled an excessive amount of air and exclaimed *"It's gone!"* The entire deliverance was probably less than sixty seconds! He never had another seizure. That's how powerful the name of Jesus is.

In a society where Satan is thought to be a mythical figure, (even by church folks) evil spirits can openly torment people in this way and get away with it. I have offered to pray for others in similar conditions only to be politely refused. People cannot see how a simple prayer can be of any help when the best drugs and or medical help can't solve the problem. We have to pray that the Lord will open their eyes.

Learning To Trust God

Early in my supernatural experiences, one night as I lay in bed before going to sleep, I began to hear demonic voices in my natural hearing. It overwhelmed me at the time. I was wondering what to do because I definitely did not want to experience that again. As I pondered the situation, a realization began to set in. I knew that the devil hates us and would kill us if he had the opportunity. I resigned myself that there was nothing that I myself could do. The only thing that protects us is the Lord. That made me aware that the Lord is with us, and we don't have to be afraid. We have to trust God.

Going In The Spirit

Many times when you are in the spirit, you encounter things that are unpleasant. You can openly encounter spirits that will try to temp you into any sin that you had previously taken part in or possibly deceive you in some other way. On one occasion I had been praying in my prayer chair and fell asleep. I then found myself waking from sleep in the spirit realm. As I looked in the spirit I saw what I thought was a tormented human soul. He held out his hand to me and said *"Hurry! take my hand, I'm going to Hades!"*. I took his hand and immediately felt as if I was moving somewhere in the spirit, so I quickly let go. He again said it even more insistently *"Hurry! Take my hand, I'm going to Hades!"*. So I again took his hand and immediately found myself moving somewhere again. This time however someone intervened and rebuked me gently like you might rebuke a child who doesn't know better. (Most likely an angel) He said *"Where do you think you're going?!"* And I again let go with the knowledge that I should not do that again. I honestly believe that I thought I was going to help someone from going to Hades by taking their hand.

We have to be aware in the spirit and realize that there are deceiving spirits who will try to lead us the wrong way if they can. That's why the Bible says...

Dear friends, do not believe every spirit, but test the spirits to see whether they are from God, because many false prophets have gone out into the world. This is how you can recognize the spirit of God: Every spirit that acknowledges that Jesus Christ has come in the flesh is from God.
(1 John 4:1-2)

Dark Places

When you go into the spirit it can be one of the most exhilarating things you can experience, but sometimes you may find yourself in places and think *"How in the world did I wind up here?"* Dark places with ungodly people or demonic beings that are very unpleasant places indeed. Once I was seeking God and wound up in the spirit in some dark, barren and bleak corridor with empty rooms on either side of it. As I explored this dark place, I saw a tall skeleton like being with long stringy hair walking down a hallway away from me. I called out to him *"Hey! Get back here in Jesus' name"*. I have no idea why I did that, but he turned and slowly walked toward me.

His eyes were dead and he was completely emotionless as he grabbed me by the throat and picked me up off the ground. The next thing I knew, I was back in the natural realm.

Another time I found myself in a basement of sorts and there were people in there but I couldn't see them too well. I decided I would shine a light into the darkness to see better. When I turned on the light and shone it into the darkness the people in the darkness reacted strongly, cursing me and telling me to turn out that light! They also cowered away from the light receding further into the darkness behind them.

Experience Or Dream?

As I have mentioned, everything seems dreamlike before you have experience or understanding about these experiences. I believe that these are real places in the spirit realm that are similar to regions of captivity but more of a soulish place of influence than an actual place of bondage. If you encounter these types of places as you go into the spirit, you only have to remember two things, One, the name of Jesus and two, the blood of Jesus. If you call upon His name you will be fine. He has given his angels charge over you and although it may seem as if you are alone, you are not. His angels are ever with you and will protect you.

Binding The Devil

One day I happened to be somewhere on business where there was a man who was using the most vile language and profanity as he spoke to me. He was lacing profanity all throughout his conversation as if this was normal speaking for him. I was angry (not at the man but at his oppressor) and sought the Lord. I felt the Lord tell me to stand very close to him and just release the love of God over him from my spirit, which I did. Then the Lord told me to bind the spirit controlling his speech. When I did that, the man suddenly looked confused and couldn't talk at all hardly.

He went and found a chair and sat down to compose himself. When he began to speak again, it was normal speech.

Use Your Authority

We all encounter such things every day. I believe that because almost all of society is laced with little things that defile, we put up with it more than we have to. We get used to it because "everybody" does it or "everybody" talks that way nowadays. If you are a Christian who knows that you have authority, the devil will try to control your atmosphere for you so that you don't. If you control the atmosphere it will change people around you whether you ever have a chance to actually talk with them or not! I always try to remember to release the government of the Kingdom of Heaven over *every* place I go . I know you've heard it before but it bears repeating, be a thermostat not a thermometer!

Verily I say unto you, whatsoever ye shall bind on earth shall be bound in Heaven, and whatsoever ye shall loose on earth shall be loosed in Heaven. (Matthew 18:18)

Blowback From The Enemy

When you serve God, you have the opportunity to minister to people who are bound by everything that you can think of. It may be a sickness or a sin or an ungodly habit or relationship problem and it really is a joyful thing when we are able to help them. One thing I've learned however is that sometimes you may literally have to fight their battles. It's ok, as long as we know what's going on.

I was really seeking God and His will and trying to pray for people who needed prayer, sometimes interceding and sometimes fasting. I would seemingly out of the blue, start having the most ungodly dreams or thoughts though.

I would try to think what I had done to open this door and couldn't come up with anything. One day at a conference I happened to talk with a deliverance minister from the church we were visiting and he clued me in. When you are having ungodly dreams or temptations that you didn't open a door to, you are carrying a part of the battle of the people you are praying over or for. Interceding if you will. It is a blowback of sorts from the battle. Don't accept it as your own but still battle through to victory.

I Think I Know You

If you are a person who honors the supernatural things of God they will be manifest in your life. If you live in the supernatural you will deal with the unclean and demonic from time to time whether you seek battle or you don't. Please don't be in fear over this though. Everywhere we go we carry the authority of Heaven with us. There is no greater authority or power. Sometimes things from your past will try to reinsert themselves into your life. Spirits that you may have listened to in the past no longer influence you but they sure would like to.

One afternoon I was in the Goodwill store shopping for old picture frames. (I like old interesting frames to hold my artwork, drawings etc.) I was standing in the aisle-way just kind of looking around when I saw a young girl about sixteen years old walking toward me with the most beautiful smile on her face. I assumed she knew me from somewhere and I probably knew her, but from where? A friend of my wife's? A daughter of a friend of my wife's? I couldn't place her at all. When she got up close to me I still didn't have a clue and she still had the most lovely smile on her face when she said to me *"We miss you"*, in a demonic voice. Then she turned and walked away. I'll be honest, I was too stunned to move for a minute. Eventually I got my composure and prayed for the girl's deliverance. We are in a battle and it's better to be aware than unaware. When you are in the supernatural of God, you are going through life with your eyes open.

Angels Know How To Fight

If you have or seek spiritual sight you will soon know how awesome the angels are who surround your life. They know how to fight . All of them.

One evening I was in the spirit and fighting with some demonic thing. I was "wrestling" with him and rebuking him at the same time and I seemed to have my hands full. The battle was a stand-off. I didn't seem to be gaining any ground. As I fought, I suddenly heard someone say *"Ask the angel to fight for you"*. So I said *"angel of the Lord Please fight for me!"* Suddenly I saw the demon frantically fighting with something that I could not see. It looked like he was terrified and fighting someone invisible. It was awesome and taught me an important lesson about warfare. Ask the angels to fight for you!

More Lightening!

This testimony is more evidence and encouragement that the Lord is ever vigilant over our lives. I have seen angels as lightning a couple of times now. It's incredible to see and speaks to me of the speed and power that they possess.

Many times if I happen to wake up in the night, I will lay perfectly still and open one or both eyes and see if there are any spiritual sights to see around me. Other times I will awake and keep my eyes closed and look for spiritual sights. This night I woke up with a strange feeling that I couldn't place. I kept my eyes closed and looked around to see if I could see anything. Laying on my right side and looking towards the middle of the room, I saw what appeared to be several black and dark red veiled figures creeping up on me. They were moving very slowly and I just watched them. Because there was a veil and I couldn't see them clearly, I thought to myself *"I wonder if they are demonic?"* I then decided I would call upon the Lord and see what happened.

I began to form the words "*I rebuke you*" but while they were still only in my mind and had not yet come out of my mouth, I saw five or six flashes of lightning and the creeping figures were gone! That is how fast those angels move! That's why you can trust the Lord when He says that He will never leave you!

...I will never leave thee nor forsake thee. (Hebrews 13:5)

11

THE STRANGE AND WONDERFUL

If you have read this far, I really pray that you have been encouraged enough to seek this supernatural life in God for yourself. He doesn't make it hard. He helps us every step of the way. There are so many experiences and blessings to enjoy when you seek the deep things. Many are hard to describe and many are just strange and wonderful!

For this first encounter I have to revisit my experience with the prophecy and following confirmation of the instruction from the Lord about writing the book "How to See in the Spirit". As you know, after the Lord told me to write the book He then had Apostle Art McGuire prophesy over me to write the book and then gave me a very specific financial blessing as a confirmation that this instruction was indeed from Him. Now here is the third and final part of this event surrounding the writing of the book.

After receiving that wonderful confirmation from the Lord verifying that the word Apostle McGuire had spoken was from Him, I was content. I knew it was Him and I began the process. However there was still more apparently that the Lord wanted to do. A couple of weeks after the prophecy had been given I awoke one night and I looked around as I often do when I awake, to see what I can see. There was nothing in front of me, but something caught my eye and I craned my neck back to see what it was. There floating above our heads, not far from the headboard was a book. And the book had wings on each side...and the book was *looking* at me!

This book had two eyes right in the middle and a wing on each side and was just hovering over the bed. It was one of the strangest things I've ever seen. Originally I had thought it was a box with eyes, and I described it to my wife Gordana. Gordana in wisdom said *"maybe it's a book"*. Which I realized made a lot more sense in light of the recent events!

Symbol Of Protection

This is yet another reason why I know the angels are ever present to protect us.

Ryan Wyatt was going to be speaking in Ohio at John Belt's church and I really felt that I should go. The worship was phenomenal and the atmosphere was tangible with God's presence. I was glad I went. The great thing about going to these types of events is that the atmosphere surrounding the event seems to clothe you or come upon you when you are in it. Kind of like when Saul prophesied when he was in the presence of the prophets.

 At the end of the first day I was tired but excited. I slept well and awoke well rested the next morning. However, when I awoke there was a light blue transparent shield hanging in mid- air right next to my head at the side of the bed. It stayed there for only a few seconds before it faded from view. I believe it was divine angelic protection over my sleep.

Taking Back The Land

Sometimes there are places in our homes that just don't "feel" right. There are rooms that the kids don't want to go into or you may have weird dreams if you fall asleep there. Such was my daughter Angie's bedroom at one point. For some strange reason the room just felt different and my daughter experienced some strange dreams and just felt uncomfortable in the room.

I decided that I would let her sleep with my wife in our bed and I would sleep in her room so I could see (or feel) what was going on.

The Lord showed me some very specific stuff in the spirit (courtesy of some outside sources) and led me how to pray. I went to sleep and slept the rest of the night very well. Again, when I awoke I saw the transparent shield by my head again and this time I also saw a field of sparkling lights hovering in place at the foot of the bed. The Lord protects us in these ways even when we are not aware of it.

Incredibly Beautiful Orb

Sometimes things just show up. We aren't necessarily seeking it but God wants us to have it anyway. One night I suddenly woke up out of a dead sleep and lifted my head up to see what was above me. I knew something was there but didn't know how I knew. There, right above my head was the most beautiful translucent blue and purple orb I have ever seen. It was about the size of a cantaloupe and it was filled with what looked like a hundred golden specks of light or fire. It was awesome! I stretched out my hand toward it and when I touched it, it went into my hand. The feeling was slightly uncomfortable so I questioned the source in my mind for a brief instant. As I did I heard the words *"healing virtue"*. I then realized that I had received an impartation from the Lord.

Can Numbers Float?

I know that I have mentioned it but I will mention it again because it's important to understand. If you give a few minutes of your late night or early morning to train your eyes to see in the spirit, you will see some amazing sights. Ok, now I can continue.

One morning upon awakening I opened my eyes to see a large red number eight floating about four feet off the ground from the hallway door toward me. I watched it the whole way in amazement as it came closer and closer to me. When it was almost upon me it just disappeared!

I wondered what it could mean. I remembered reading somewhere that the number eight meant new beginnings but I didn't want to accept that *only* because that was my previous understanding. After two days of thinking about it I heard *"why don't you ask me"* in my spirit. I felt it was the Holy Spirit talking to me. So I asked Him and He said *"it means new beginnings"*. Ha! Ok I believed it now. Later in the evening at home I was telling my family about the experience with the red number eight and my daughter immediately said *"that means new beginnings!"* I said *"how in the world would you know that?"* And she responded *"We just learned that at school!"*

Cool! I love confirmation! And new beginnings!

I have also seen a number three floating toward me in like manner but I didn't have a clear understanding of what the significance of it was. But it lets me know that God is involved and that's the most important thing. However, it's *really* nice to see evidence of His involvement and that's why I again encourage you to look so you may see! In Brenda McDonald's book "Dream Meanings Dictionary" she says the number three represents the Trinity and a strong three fold cord bond. I'll take it!

Living Creatures

One night past midnight I happened to open my eyes. I wasn't trying to see anything but had a brief glance of a subtle shift of some kind in the atmosphere of some kind to my right. I watched that area for about forty-five seconds and the sight then became more clear. At first as I began to focus, it looked like a horse's head. But then it became clear that it was some other type of creature who was definitely not a horse but whose head was shaped like a horse's head. As this being became aware that I could see him he began to move and flew past me as he flew away. He was approximately thirty feet long and moved as if he was swimming through water.

I had no fear whatsoever and no sense that this being was anything demonic. I believe that he was some sort of living creature and was there just watching over us like the angels do!

If you pursue spiritual sight or the supernatural things of God you may experience things like this. You don't have to be in fear though. The Holy Spirit will bear witness of what is of Him and what is not. Listen for God's voice and you can navigate the supernatural realms fearlessly!

For God has not given us the spirit of fear, but of power, and of love, and of a sound mind. (2 Timothy 1:7)

One Starry Night

One night I was lying in bed and staring up at the ceiling before going to sleep. As I laid there suddenly I became aware that I was not seeing the bedroom ceiling but was seeing the stars instead! I said to myself *"but I'm inside the house, how am I seeing stars?"* A voice spoke in my spirit and said *"because you are seeing in the spirit"*

A Brief Testimony

Only this very evening as I am writing this, I became very excited to hear a testimony of someone who had read my book "How to See in the Spirit". They said that they had done some of the "exercises" to help increase spiritual sight and while lying in bed they had also seen the stars above them rather than the ceiling! Thank You Jesus!

Swirling Lights And Colors

One of the most common things I experience in my room at night or in the morning when I look to see what I can see is movement of light in various shapes and various ways. It's not an overwhelming light but rather very subtle and you have to look for it and then it gradually becomes more apparent. Also colors changing before my eyes, almost like spiritual clouds that move into different colors or morph into different colors, one after the other. Usually the colors I see are different shades of blue and purple and sometimes a very striking green color as well.

I have listened to many people talk about angels and some have said that these shifting colors we see are actually angels called Cashmillion Angels. (I'm not sure if I spelled their name correctly)

Since vague swirling lights and colors seem to be a common thing for me, I would guess that they will be for you as well if you are engaging this gift of sight. Enjoy their presence.

The Fire Of God

One of the most awesome things I have experienced while in prayer or while waiting on the Lord is the manifestation of fire next to me, around me or coming down upon me. I believe this is a sanctification sent from God to allow us to carry or move in greater things. Ask God for His fire.

Most of the handful of times that I have experienced this, I have actually been asking the Lord to sanctify me. I have prayed for His cleansing fire to come upon me and make me clean and while praying that I will also envision in my mind, angels dumping buckets of fire over my head or my being covered in fire.

One night while praying this way a pillar of fire appeared behind my chair and at first I only slowly leaned my head back into it. After I realized it would not hurt me I began leaning my head back into the fire then bringing it out, over and over. I know it did something significant for me. This is also something I would encourage you to ask for as well.

Angel I know You're There

You know the angels are around us even when we don't see them. He has given His angels charge over us and they obey the Lord. We still like to see them though. It is an encouragement to see God's angels. It's a real blessing and uplifting experience. I will let the angels know sometimes (more than sometimes) that I want to see them or some evidence of them and sometimes they will respond.

I have told them on occasion *"angel please just take your sword and poke it through the veil so I can see it for a second"*, and sometimes they have done that. I wonder sometimes what they think about those types of requests. Do they laugh and shake their heads or do they understand our need to feel connected to the things of Heaven? Only a few days ago I woke up in the night and right next to the bed I saw a sword hilt and part of the blade. I wonder if it's the same angel that I'm always asking to poke his sword through the veil for me. Maybe he just beat me to the punch!

Be sensitive to the fact that the angels are around you. Not just with your sight but with your other senses as well. How many times have you been praying and felt a cool breeze on your face? See? That's the angel refreshing you as you pray.

Angelic Energy

My wife Gordana and I had gone to the hospital one evening to visit and pray for someone and were walking through the hallways to the elevator. As we got the a corner in the hallway, we both felt a very real, very tangible force field of some sort that we walked right through. It appeared to be several feet wide and a couple of feet thick. I asked her *"did you feel that?!"* She indeed had. We walked back and forth through it several times before it was no longer there!

Along that same line, one night about nine pm I went for an hour long prayer walk around the neighborhood. Towards the end of my walk, my prayer became more intense and I was asking the Lord to do something extreme. I really didn't care what the Lord would do, I just wanted it to be extreme. When I was about two blocks from home, I began to hear a humming that gradually got louder. I also began to feel some sort of energy on or around me. It felt like the atmosphere around me was vibrating.

Even though I had been praying for God to do something extreme, as this began to happen I found myself looking around to see if there was some electric transformer nearby that I hadn't seen before. As I did this the experience faded within seconds. It's really funny how we can have the most supernatural events happen and we still try to rationalize them and explain them by natural means. I really think that we (I) need to look to the supernatural explanation first, and then if that's not it we can explore natural explanations. It would probably keep wonderful manifestations of God from slipping away from us.

The Gold Dust Phenomenon

Is anybody else provoked to jealousy by Joshua Mills? I know I sure am. The first time I had heard about people being covered in gold dust I thought it was really cool. The first time I had seen it I was stunned.

Seeing Joshua getting covered in more and more gold dust as he worshipped or preached only made me cry out *"I want that!"*

My wife's friend Kim has kind of mentored us in things supernatural over the last few years. Taking us to conferences and giving us "meaty" things of God to chew on. Kim was also prophesied over by Bonnie Chavda, given a mantle and told that she would minister in the glory like Ruth Ward Heflin. For those of you who may not know, Ruth was pretty much the "original" one to experience the gold dust when she preached. (Or at least the one we know about)

When Kim began to come over for fellowship, many times we would see little flecks of gold dust appear on her face as she talked about the Lord. Sometimes it was quite a lot! Eventually it began to spread just a little. One time my wife also had three little flecks of gold on her and I had one little dot of gold on me.

The last time I got any gold on me seemed very much random as I was not doing anything spiritual, I was just getting a cup of coffee. I was standing at the sink when my wife said *"you have a little piece of gold on your face"*, and she pointed to it. Then she called our daughter over to see it and as they were looking at it, it disappeared!

Signs and wonders. Little signs that make you wonder.

Heaven's Bible Highlighter

My wife Gordana was given an intercessor's mantle by the Lord back in 2011 at a Bill Johnson / Randy Clark conference. Since that time she has experienced the most extreme and awesome manifestations of God's power. One of the little things that the Lord does for her now is to highlight scriptures as she reads the Bible. As she reads along, many times a little diamond or sapphire or ruby will appear and lay on a verse. Sometimes for just a moment, sometimes more.

Many times the entire page will be covered in gemstones as she reads. She will ask us *"Can you see them?!"*

I purposely have not shared very much about my families' testimony or the things that they have experienced because at some point I would like them to share these things for themselves and in their own words. It is really a blessing to watch the Lord bless my family and I am looking forward to that time.

A Beautiful Crystal Goblet

One morning recently I woke up and just kind of laid there talking to my wife who was already up and getting ready for work. As I laid there on my side with my face turned toward the middle of the room, suddenly a small hole or portal opened before me in the atmosphere quite close to my face.

My reaction was *"what is that?"* As I lay there looking at this portal, suddenly a hand reached through holding a beautiful *crystal goblet* putting it close to my face as if handing it to me. I didn't immediately know what to do. How do you accept something from the spirit realm when you are not in the spirit but the natural? I heard in my spirit...by faith. So I took it by faith and drank it. When you receive things of God by faith you will be blessed.

Fragrances of Heaven

The spiritual sense of smell is a real blessing. You can smell unclean things of the enemy which help you know what's going on or how to pray and you can smell the beautiful fragrances of Heaven. One evening back the early months of 2013, I was working at the computer when my wife called to me. *"It smells like flowers in here"*. She was down the hallway in the kitchen area. I went in there and sure enough there was a fragrance in there of flowers. (as I am typing this it is manifesting again)

We tried to investigate the source but could not find one. The smell seemed to be around her but not on her. We soon verified this as she decided to come into the room where I had been and the fragrance followed her. We soon realized that this beautiful fragrance would follow her as she went through the house. After about an hour it was gone.

One Sunday morning as we were on our way to church we were asking the Lord to manifest the smell of the "oil of the Holy Spirit" and almost immediately we smelled a strong smell of oil that actually smelled to me like cooking oil.

Another time as I was driving I was singing along with DC Talk's 'In The Light" when I suddenly smelled a strong vanilla or caramel smell. It was quite strange but quite nice.om

God's Power To Heal

Our God is a healing God. It is His nature to bring restoration to the lives of the sick and broken. I am so very happy for that! I had injured my rotator cuff several years ago and the pain during the day, I could live with, but at night it was hard to get a good night's sleep. I had to lay on my stomach with my arm at a very weird angle for me to be able to sleep. If I happened to move during the night, as I often did, I would wake up from the pain. It ranged from dull to sharp and everything in between.

I had been sleeping that way for *two years*. I needed healing. At the Ryan Wyatt event we went to in Ohio, there was a time of prayer in which Ryan called for people who needed healing to raise their hands and then those around them should pray for them. Well, I had raised my hand and there were about four people around me that first prayed for me. The couple to my right, Ken and Linda from Flint Michigan both laid hands on me and prayed as well as others.

I remember that Linda would pray and then ask me to check if I was healed yet. She wasn't giving up.
She had done it several times and I just closed my eyes and felt everyone's hands of my shoulders. When only one hand remained I thought it was probably Linda's since she was the most aggressive toward my healing. But when I opened my eyes to see who it was, it was no one. No one in the natural was touching me. I was completely healed.

Is It Really That Simple?

A man I had only known for a week or so had badly injured his foot. He had smashed it in an accident and now had nerve damage. He had been going to therapy but was in great pain. I had been talking with him about prayer and the power of God to heal and he knew something of God's power because he had experienced it before.

I said *"let me pray for your foot"* and he said ok. I don't think he actually expected me to do it right then and there, but I just knelt down and laid my hand on his foot and commanded his foot to be healed and the nerves to be made new in Jesus' name. Just like Todd White! Actually I thought about Todd White when I was doing it, that's why I mentioned him. As I prayed he said *"there's something moving in my foot. It feels like electricity going through my foot."* I said check it out. He began moving and walking on it and checking it and he was amazed. He looked at me seriously and said *"Is it really that simple?"* I said *"Yes, it is"*.

Orbs, Oil, And David Hogan

We all love (missionary to Mexico) David Hogan in our house. We watch him on Youtube on a regular basis and many of the programs we watch we have seen many times. One evening Gordana and Angie and I were all seated by the computer watching a really spectacular teaching and message by David Hogan. After the message they went into a time of worship and we all lifted our hands in worship just like the folks on the monitor.

Angie felt something strange on one of her hands and realized that she had oil on her palm. Supernatural oil appeared during the worship. Gordana who sees fairly openly in the spirit realm, also saw two orbs of light floating around us. It was a very good day.

Thick Dark Clouds

This particular trip into the realm of the Kingdom was a great learning experience of many levels. One night I awoke to find myself moving through the spirit realm. I was flying through a type of semi cloudy atmosphere. With a vast expanse in front of me. I became aware that in the distance was a huge grouping(s) of thick dark clouds with all kinds of light moving within them. The lights ranged from beautiful colorful orbs of light of every size to flashes of light and other lights and colors within the clouds that I can't quite describe to you.

I approached these clouds, closer and closer until I was almost upon them, then I found myself in them. I was suddenly in a very large open place, very light and peaceful. I walked down a wide promenade of sorts. There were benches around where you could sit and little tables as well. I was aware somehow that this was some area of Heaven. I continued to walk along in wonder, enjoying the sights as I went.

Not far from me I saw a black man seated at a table and I got an idea to ask him a question. Knowing that I was in Heaven, I got the idea to ask him if he knew a certain person that had recently died, and if they had made it to Heaven.

The person I asked about had lived a very wicked life most of his life. Chasing after lusts of the flesh and worldly pursuits openly seemingly without shame or remorse. I felt almost certain he was most likely *not* in Heaven even though

towards the end of his life he began to *appear* to act differently.
The man at the table said *"Oh yes. I know him. He's up here in an area called special blessings"*.

I was shocked to be honest. And then he told me where it was and how to get there.

This trip into the heavenly realm made me very aware that God is more merciful than we can imagine. The Lord had somehow brought this man to repentance. I then knew that virtually anyone can be saved.

Even More Lightning still!

The Lord knows I love His lightning. I tell Him every time I see lightning how much I appreciate it and how beautiful it is. I will stand outside under the eaves of our house during rainstorms so I can watch the lightning without my view being impeded. I have no fear of it, only awe and wonder. I firmly believe there is a spiritual reason behind it and it is then manifested in the natural realm That's why I also ask the Lord to let some of that angelic blessing (of their presence) come upon our home.

One evening a couple of years ago my son Matt came in the house and said *"dad you have got to come and see this!"* I followed Matt outside to a very surreal manifestation of lightening going on. The weather was nice and there was lots of cloud cover but no rain whatsoever. Matt suggested we get lawn chairs and set them up in the drive way so that we could enjoy this "lightning show".

We got the lawn chairs out and parked them in the middle of the driveway where the view was best. My wife Gordana thought we were nuts. For almost two hours we sat there and watched *thousands* of lightning bolts reach across the sky. There was no break between them. The lightning came in waves over our house, with as many as fifteen to twenty "fingers" of lightning reaching over our house at one time.

This "hand" of lightning reached over us so many times and so close, I believe that God was telling us something.

There was lightning in the far distance, in the near distance and right over us continually for the entire time. It was the most awesome display I have ever seen in the natural realm. It really inspired us to think about how awesome our God is.

The reason I am talking about this "natural" display is because many times God speaks to us in the natural things around us. Whether it is a rainstorm or a time we keep noticing on the clock or an offhanded remark someone says that seems to fit seamlessly into our lives and situations. We have to keep an awareness about us if we really want to see all God has for us.

This Belongs To You

I am passionate that people learn about what is available in God. That is the purpose behind this book and also my previous book, How to See in the Spirit. I know that once people really get a revelation of how real God is and how much He loves them, it will cause everything to make sense. People will find that they have a divine purpose that is more awesome and satisfying than anything they have ever dreamed of.

These testimonies in this book are a tool of sorts to inspire you to look deeper than you ever have. This is all for you, every bit of it. There is nothing that God has done for me that He won't do for you too. This is my desire for you.

12

SUPERNATURAL RESOURCES

Having now read some of the wonderful experiences that the Lord has allowed me and my family to encounter, I pray that you too have a deeper desire to go further and experience not just more but all that the Kingdom of Heaven has to offer. As you may have noticed from reading this book, many of the supernatural things of God I have experienced were born out of testimonies that I have heard and laid hold of for myself.

Every day I seem to hear more and more great testimonies from people all over the world whom God is touching or using or blessing in some wonderful way. It's like a snowball of sorts. Here's what I mean. As I began to learn about the deeper things, I would hear Ryan Wyatt, who I knew about, mention Bob Jones, who would then mention Gary Oates, then I went to a conference with Gary in Moravian falls.

At the conference I met someone named Terry who told me about Curry Blake who then mentioned David Hogan. David

Hogan then told a great testimony about Ana Mendez, and on and on it goes.

Since this journey began for me it has taken a couple of years to even learn of people whose lives have really come to inspire me. That's why I wanted to include at the end of this book, a listing of names, places and resources that will bless you to know about if you are pursuing this supernatural lifestyle. These lists are far from comprehensive.

Anointed People

Ok. These people aren't just anointed, they are also people I happen to like very much. They all move in miraculous power and I want you to know who they are. You can research all these resources online and find loads of stuff.

Bruce Allen... A modern day Enoch who has taught me so much about walking in the supernatural things of God. Solid and Christ-like character

Sadhu Sundar Selvaraj... Lives a life of walking in the miraculous and power of God. So many incredible testimonies about his life I wouldn't know where to start.

David Hogan... Carries amazing power and he's not afraid to use it. Has seen or participated in every sort of miracle you can think of...literally.

Joseph D. Hogan (Jody)... Also carries amazing power from God. The atmosphere around him is tangible.

Heidi Baker.. So full of love. Incredible passion for the lost and hurting. Sees miracles of Biblical proportion as a lifestyle. If you know Heidi, you know she has no plan "B".

Todd White... Bold and unrelenting. He knows who he is and he inspires you to know who you are and then live it.

Dr. Lester Sumrall..* No nonsense but compassion that caused him to live for others. Power. The first person who ever knocked me down by just touching me.

Benny Hinn... Knows how to bring people into the glory. Also has tangible power in him.

*This list has been seriously amended due to some people not desiring to be listed here in my book. I have removed the vast amount of people that were in the book and just kept the few who I know personally or who know my intentions for having listed them.

Recommended Reading

These are all books that I have read and studied. Many of these books I have read several times. There is a literal anointing on these books to convey and impart the truth that they carry. These books cover a range from spiritual sight to healing to moving in the supernatural and more.

Open My Eyes Lord by Gary Oates
The School of Seers by Jonathan Welton
God's Supernatural Power by Bobby Conner

The Seer Anointing by Brenda McDonald
Eyes That See by Patricia King
Spiritual Revolution by Patricia King

How to See in the Spirit World by Mel Bond
Releasing God's Anointing by Mel Bond
Understanding Your Worst Enemy by Mel Bond

Dancing With Angels 1,2 & 3 by Kevin Basconi
Glory by Ruth Ward Heflin
Quantum Fasting by Emerson Ferrell

Supernatural Believing by Emerson Ferrell
Becoming the Master's Key by Emerson Ferrell
Immersed in Him by Emerson Ferrell

Regions of Captivity by Ana Mendez Ferrell
Shaking the Heavens by Ana Mendez Ferrell
Iniquity by Ana Mendez Ferrell

Gazing into Glory by Dr. Bruce Allen
Translation by Faith by Dr. Bruce Allen
When Heaven Invades Earth by Bill Johnson
The Ultimate Treasure Hunt by Kevin Dedmon

Good Morning Holy Spirit by Benny Hinn

Angels on Assignment by Roland Buck
The Supernatural Ways of Royalty by Kris Vallotton

The Veil by Blake Healy

Visions, Visitations and the Voice of God
                    By Lyn Packer
The Normal Supernatural Christian Life
                    By Aliss Cresswell

The Prophetic Promise of the Seventh Day
                    By Dr. Bruce Allen

~ A lot of the books I have listed have to do with developing spiritual sight. The reason for this is because spiritual sight is a gateway of sorts into other things in the Kingdom and this allows you to navigate and understand other things more readily.

Although I have listed only a few books, I could have listed many, many more that have really blessed me and taught me. My personal library is probably about three hundred books that are pretty much all on these topics.

Websites and other resources

Pretty much all of the people mentioned here have resources that you can get online. Whether in book or PDF, or MP3s, CD's, or streaming live broadcasts and Youtube videos. Here are a few sites that I go to again and again to drink from. I have listed some of my favorites.

Elijah List
http://www.elijahlist.com/index.php

Fresh prophetic words, conferences and other resources.

John G. Lake Ministries
http://www.jglm.org/

Curry Blake has some of the best teaching on healing the sick available. Check out his Divine Healing Technician course.

Sid Roth's It's Supernatural!
http://sidroth.org/

Sid Roth is almost last but not least! His weekly program and the archive of past radio and television programs of all things supernatural of God are a must for anyone desiring to live a supernatural lifestyle. Uplifting and encouraging, Sid will provoke you to jealousy! I cannot recommend this program enough! It is awesome!

Sadhu Sundar Selvaraj

http://www.jesusministries.org/

Brother Sadhu is a man who walks with God in intimacy and he will show you how to do the same. He has excellent resources to teach you and inspire you and equip you to live a supernatural life in God. Awesome Materials, DVDs on spiritual sight.

Trust Jesus

If you have never made Jesus Lord of your life I would encourage you to do so now. Just pray this simple prayer in faith as you voice your commitment to Him.

Dear Jesus, Thank you for dying on the cross and spilling your blood to pay the price for my sins. I repent, I turn myself toward you and receive you as my Savior and Lord. Please fill me with your Spirit and use me for your glory. In your name I pray, amen.

If you have sincerely prayed that prayer, the Spirit of the living God now resides within you. You are a new creation! Read His Word and talk to Him every day! He desires to give you a life beyond anything you have ever hoped for!

GOD BLESS YOU!

ABOUT THE AUTHOR

Michael Van Vlymen was born in Blue Island, IL in 1958. He grew up the son of Pastor / Missionary parents and has lived in many places including Brazil, SA. Michael is a writer who enjoys sharing and teaching about the things God has shown him and an artist who specializes in portraits and spiritual themes. Michael is also a musician who enjoys playing the guitar. Michael lives with his family in Carmel, IN. USA

Also by Michael Van Vlymen
How To See In The Spirit
A practical guide on engaging the spirit realm.

Printed in Great Britain
by Amazon